Also by George Foreman

George Foreman's Big Book of
Grilling, Barbecue, and Rotisserie
(with Barbara Witt)

George Foreman's Knock-Out-the-Fat
Barbecue and Grilling Cookbook
(with Cherie Calbom)

George Foreman's Guide to Life
(with Linda Kulman)

By George
(with Joel Engel)

George Foreman's
INDOOR GRILLING MADE EASY

More Than 100 Simple, Healthy Ways to Feed Family and Friends

GEORGE FOREMAN
with Kathryn Kellinger

Simon & Schuster
New York London Toronto Sydney

SIMON & SCHUSTER
Rockefeller Center
1230 Avenue of the Americas
New York, NY 10020

SIMON & SCHUSTER and colophon are registered trademarks
of Simon & Schuster, Inc.

For information about special discounts for bulk purchases,
please contact Simon & Schuster Special Sales:
1-800-456-6798 or business@simonandschuster.com

Designed by Joel Avirom and Jason Snyder
Design assistant: Meghan Day Healey

Interior illustrations © 2004 by Laura Coyle

Manufactured in the United States of America

10

Library of Congress Cataloging-in-Publication Data

Foreman, George.
    George Foreman's indoor grilling made easy : more than 100 simple, healthy ways to
feed family and friends / George Foreman with Kathryn Kellinger.
        p. cm.
    Includes index.
    1. Barbecue cookery. I. Kellinger, Kathryn. II. Title.

TX840.B3F655 2004
641.5'784—dc22   2004056616

ISBN-13: 978-0-7432-6674-1
ISBN-10:   0-7432-6674-9

To Mary Foreman,
for her constant dedication
and willingness to always be there
and take the first taste.

Acknowledgments

My thanks to all the great folks out there who've used my grill over the years and have been kind enough to share with me their cooking secrets; to my literary agent, Miriam Altshuler; to my longtime friends and colleagues at Salton, Gary Ragan and especially Samantha Dreimann, who introduced me to the best chefs in the world; to writer Kathryn Kellinger, whose sense of humor—and taste—never failed her; to Jennifer Martelly and Claudette Foreman, my champions around the grill; to Suki Hertz, nutrition wizard; and finally, to my only publisher, David Rosenthal, and the other folks at Simon & Schuster—editor Beth Wareham, Rica Allannic, and Elizabeth Hayes—who made this book happen.

Contents

Introduction

My daughter Freeda calls me the Ultimate Mr. Mom—it might be the title I'm most proud of, and, in some ways, it's been the most hard-won. With ten children ranging in age from four (George VI) to thirty (my daughter Michi), it takes some pretty fancy footwork to keep a fast-moving family happy and well fed. Starting with my toddler, who likes to eat a little bit throughout the day. (He, like all little ones, can be finicky, but I find that most kids will eat anything as long as you cut their food up small enough.) Then I've got meals and snacks for my teenagers and their friends who are just getting in from school or needing some high-energy fuel before heading off to practice. As for my wife, my older children, and myself, we're looking for grown-up good food that not only tastes great but is in line with our commitment to healthy choices. Between kids, schools, careers, and a heavyweight training schedule, the Foremans are a big, fast-moving family. Getting dinner on the table could be an endurance event, but instead of going ten rounds in the kitchen, I've got the 1–2 punch for fast and easy: *George Foreman's Indoor Grilling Made Easy*.

These days, my family is no different from any other (although it's probably bigger than most); fast-paced schedules make putting good simple food on the table more of a gold-medal challenge than ever before. In this, my third cookbook, I aim to map out the simplest ways to feed your family healthy and delicious food using the cooking method that makes it easiest—The Lean Mean Grilling Machine, the first indoor grill built with sloped plates so the fat just runs right off. Whether I'm making myself lunch or cooking dinner for the whole family, indoor grilling is the key to a fast, fuss-free meal. The recipes that follow are easy enough for beginner cooks but delicious enough for the most experienced eaters—like me!

For my super-sized family, cooking is a team sport. We use time in the kitchen as a time to be together, work together, and make plans. Some of my kids are in school while others are working on their own careers, so we really look forward to the times when we can all be together, putting dinner on the table. Sundays are what we look forward to most, when a big family dinner immediately follows church. I hear people complaining that they can't coordinate their family's hectic schedules, and, with a family as big and busy as mine, I know it's not easy. But we're committed to these times together—it's that important to us. The Lean Mean Grilling Machine means we can spend less time cooking dinner and more time at the table, enjoying it.

Besides fast and easy, I want food that's healthy. My philosophy toward healthy eating has been developed during my long career as an athlete. I've seen food fads come and go . . . and then come and go again! From my first Olympic Gold Medal in Mexico City back in 1968 to my second heavyweight title at the age of forty-five, I've had a bird's-eye view of diets that promised everything from peak performance to miracle weight loss. That year at the Olympics I remember some athletes believed that eating nothing but liver would help deliver first-place performances. Imagine! Since then there've been egg yolks, egg whites, no fat, low fat, high fat, high carbs, low carbs, and no carbs. I've tried some of them and seen my weight rise and fall along the way. While I had the discipline to capture the heavyweight championship twice, I found that when I wasn't training, junk food was irresistible. I grew up poor and hungry, so losing weight was a problem I never dreamed of having. But I'd pack on the pounds and then lose them the same way each time; dieting and intense training in the gym whenever I prepared for a fight.

I know now that the best way to eat is also the simplest—plenty of fresh fruits and vegetables, lean meats, and moderate portions. My no-fad, three-meals-a-day approach keeps me, and the whole Foreman crew, in tip-top shape with just a little bit of time spent in the kitchen. As head chef, I make sure that each meal is made up of protein: skinless chicken breasts, fresh fish, or my favorite, lean beef, along with platters of grilled vegetables and salad. My ideal meal is simply prepared, cooked in minutes, and leaves me and my family satisfied but not too full.

The Lean Mean Grilling Machine is the best tool I know for cooking healthful, knock-out-the-fat meals in a flash. Indoor grilling means there are no coals to light and next to no preparation—it's fast and flame free. Since the grill cooks both sides of everything at once, food is finished in no time flat. And cleanup is as simple as a damp sponge or paper towel. What you're left with is great-tasting, well-cooked food with no smoke but with those great-looking grill marks. The grill's patented sloped design means that excess fat drips away. I am the world champ of feeding the family, and nothing gets me out of the kitchen faster than the Lean Mean Grilling Machine.

I finished building my family's dream house a while back, and one of the things I love best about it is that there's a kitchen attached to my home gym.

Now I'm able to integrate a quick meal into my lengthy workouts and that means indoor grilling. A little grilled chicken or a protein-packed piece of fish along with a salad takes only minutes away from my workout but gives me the energy to keep on training. When the boys are working out I make sure there's a platter of grilled vegetables for them to snack on. As a father, I love having the kids and their friends front and center, and I love making sure they've got plenty of good food to eat.

And my kids love to help out in the kitchen (I haven't met a kid who doesn't), so we've got a team approach to getting dinner on the table. The great thing about indoor grilling is that it's the perfect way to get the kids cooking—there's no open flame or spattering oil to worry about, so it gives the kids a chance to actually cook dinner themselves! I can coach from the corner while George V, my thirteen-year-old, serves up our favorite Do-Anything Lemon Chicken Breasts, or while my sixteen-year-old, George IV, whips up quesadillas for his friends. Even my four-year-old, George VI, gets into the game—he's the salad king—now that organic spinach and greens are sold pre-washed and ready to go. Nothing makes me happier than spending time together—a little time to make dinner, and a lot of time to eat it.

I like to cook fast and I like to cook delicious, and these recipes help me do it. Everywhere I go, any time I meet people, they tell me how much they love the grill. I've met kids who've never cooked anything before going off to college, where they met their first Lean Mean Grilling Machine—they discovered that they could make a fast dinner for their friends and that they loved doing it. I've even met world-famous chefs who tell me that, in the off-hours, when it's just them and their families, they rely on the Lean Mean Grilling Machine for fast, delicious meals. I'm proud that the grill and the book offer something for everyone—from kitchen champ to featherweight amateurs, everyone loves cooking on the Lean Mean Grilling Machine.

The recipes in this book can get anyone in the kitchen, cooking like a pro. *George Foreman's Indoor Grilling Made Easy* is just that—recipes that deliver fast and flavorful results and are easy enough for beginner cooks, but delicious enough for everyone. Whether you're cooking for one or for a whole crowd, whether you've never cooked before or are a seasoned pro, these recipes offer the broad view of quick and easy indoor grilling. From a gaggle of grilled cheese sandwiches to the exotic flavors of Southeast Asia, these are the recipes that have been the most useful to our family—quick midweek suppers, panini and burgers that the kids can't seem to get enough of, and tasty, protein-packed dinners for grown-ups watching their waistlines. These recipes cover all the ground the Foreman family needs to keep everyone well fed and on their way. Cooking for the people you love is one of life's greatest gifts, and if you're as fortunate as I've been, you've got a whole hungry army waiting for supper.

A WORD ABOUT NUTRITIONAL VALUES PER SERVING

After each recipe you'll find a breakdown of the nutritional properties of each dish. Some people live by the numbers, but I don't. Like I've said before, I believe in doing everything in moderation, which to me means eating smaller portions of all kinds of foods, always paired with lots of vegetables. Try to find some balance over the course of your day: If you splurge on a big cheeseburger for lunch, choose something lighter for dinner, such as a simple piece of grilled fish over wilted greens. If you don't know a lot about healthy eating and nutrition, you can use these numbers as a good starting point. Remember, kids and adults who are very active require more fuel, so head for heartier recipes to satisfy them.

GEORGE'S BIG 5 KEEP-IT-SIMPLE GRILLING RULES

1 Food Comes First. Whether you're stocking the fridge for the weekend, or stopping at the supermarket on the way home from work to pick up things for the evening supper, train to win by developing a food-shopping strategy. The great thing about indoor grilling is that it helps you get dinner on the table with only a few simple ingredients, so plan ahead to have those ingredients on hand and come out swinging when the bell rings (the dinner bell, that is).

2 Boneless Is Best. A bone-in piece of meat takes longer on the grill, since the meat closest to the bone takes longer than the rest of the meat. Not only does boneless cook faster, it cooks evenly and is juicy throughout.

3 Thin Is Better Than Thick. And not just when it comes to waistlines. When buying meat or fish for the grill, leave the double-cut pork chops or thick slab of tuna for the outdoor grill. For meat that's juicy on the inside and crisp but not too crisp on the outside, use the cuts recommended in the recipes.

4 Add Flavor First. Don't leave seasoning to be done at the table—take a lesson from championship chefs and make it a round-one event. Marinate, rub with spices, or simply season with salt and pepper, but do it before the food hits the grill for the best cooked-in flavor.

5 Keep It Neat. I set out my ingredients ahead of time, next to the grill. I use a tray to park things until I need them, and then I keep a platter on the other side of the grill for the finished food. A mini assembly line keeps things moving fast and easy.

The Grill

At this point I've heard hundreds of stories from folks who tell me that the Lean Mean Grilling Machine has saved the day for them. From vacation rental houses where the kitchen just didn't work to college dorm rooms with no kitchen at all, the grill can be cooked on and lived off.

I've got a friend with a big fancy yacht who cooks shrimp on the grill when he's out at sea and serves jazzy finger food with cocktails. My daughter has a friend with a custom-built chef-style kitchen—she hardly ever uses her expensive oven but makes herself a high-protein, low-carb dinner on the grill most nights. I've also heard about summer camps with rows of Lean Mean Grilling Machines lined up to grill veggie burgers for the kids.

And I just love the firemen who grill big group dinners at the firehouse. What all these folks love about indoor grilling is the same thing I love about it: it's convenient, it does it all, and it makes food with who-doesn't-love-it flavor.

The Foreman family is the extreme version of most American families—lots of kids with lots to do means that time is everything. We want to sit down to dinner together, but we don't have hours and hours to make it happen. Shopping, prepping, and cooking *have* to be easy so that we can get down to the business of a fun family life.

The grill is always ready to go. We keep it on the kitchen counter so startup is as easy as plugging it in. I'll marinate some chicken or beef before leaving in the morning so that when I come home all I have to do is turn on the grill and dinner is ten minutes away. I'll turn on the grill while I take things out of the fridge so it's preheated when I'm ready to cook (about 5 minutes). I keep a heavyweight supply of salad greens or grill-ready vegetables on hand, and I've got a complete, healthy, and delicious meal on the table, with time and energy to spare.

TEMPERATURE TALK

If your grill does not have a temperature control function, follow the instructions included with the grill. Depending upon its size, each grill requires between five to ten minutes to reach its maximum temperature. Your handy instruction manual will tell you everything you need to know.

We use the grill for almost every mealtime situation. From breakfast bacon for the boys to a lean lunch for the ladies, I can cook up a stick-to-your-ribs steak, a downright elegant main-course salad, or even a typical sit-down dinner for ten very hungry kids (not to mention their big hungry dad). Even dessert gets the grill treatment, turning fruit into a sweet but healthy finish to our family meals. I guess we haven't figured out how to do soup yet, but you can bet I'm workin' on it!

Thanks to the grill's fat-reducing design, unwanted fat drips away from food, leaving you with great taste, healthier food, and a cleanup that's a snap. The nonstick surface means that a wipe-down with a damp sponge or paper towel after a scraping with the handy tool that's included with the grill is all you need to keep things clean. (Do it while the grill is still warm from cooking and it couldn't be easier.) If I'm cooking something with cheese, I'll always pump up the nonstick properties with a quick spritz of nonstick spray to make sure that cleanup stays easy. The drip tray can go right in the dishwasher or have a soapy rinse in the sink and you're ready to go again. Indoor grilling couldn't be simpler.

Tools of the Trade

I know lots of folks who've got a gadget in their kitchen for every little task. I'm not one of 'em. I keep it real with a kitchen that's stocked with good basic tools. Since indoor grilling lets you cook everywhere, even places where you might not be able to otherwise, it's designed, as are the recipes in this book, to make gadgets and tools unnecessary. Here's what I've got in my kitchen:

Measuring Cups and Spoons They really do take the guesswork out of following a recipe. If you don't have them in your kitchen, make estimates based on the total number of ounces in a container—in other words, a quart of milk has 4 cups in it, so 1 cup of milk would be one-quarter of the whole quart. It's a great way to help kids develop their math skills.

Tongs Spring-loaded (they stay open when not being squeezed) tongs are every grill master's best friend. I use 'em for movin' hot food—on and off the grill. They're easy on cooked meat—they don't pierce like a fork does and cause all that flavorful juice to flow out. Just make sure they're not metal, which can scratch the grill; heat-resistant plastic works well, instead. For cleanup, I use them as heatproof extensions of my hand to hold a balled-up moist paper towel for wiping down the still-warm grill. If you don't have tongs, a good old spatula (again not metal) will do the job just fine.

A Good Sharp Knife For my purposes, this can be the most expensive chef's knife available, or a folding picnic knife. Just as long as the blade is sharp and long enough for the job.

Brush When I want to slick on some olive oil or brush on a glaze before grilling, a little pastry brush does the job neatly, and it lets me put just the right amount on. These are available in any kitchen store, and even most supermarkets. Truth be told, you could just as easily buy a wood-handled paintbrush at a hardware store. They work just the same. Give the brush a quick wash in warm soapy water before drying in the dish drain.

Mallet I use the mallet to pound out paper-thin cutlets. I put boneless chicken breasts or boneless pork chops between two pieces of waxed paper and pound them to a ½-inch thickness. Not only does this cut their time on the grill down to almost nothing, but it makes the meat more delicious in salads, or tacos, or however I'm serving it. If you don't have a meat mallet, use the bottom of a heavy skillet or a rolling pin.

Skewers Indoor grilling is great for kebabs, brochettes, and satays—in other words, all manner of meat on sticks (and fruit too). Bamboo skewers are best (metal gets hot and can burn you), and they are sold at the supermarket in plastic bags. I've always got a supply of skewers on hand. I never know when the urge for a kebab will strike, so I am always prepared!

Salad Spinner Ours gets almost as much mileage as the Lean Mean Grilling Machine. The spinner is the best way to rinse and dry leafy greens, and the salad greens can also be refrigerated in the spinner after the collected water has been spilled out. With clean greens in the fridge, it's nothing but convenient to grill up a little steak and salad.

Shallow Nonreactive Dish or Bowl In other words, glass. I use my heatproof glass baking dish constantly, for marinating meats and for refrigerating leftovers. My other favorite way to marinate meat is in a large resealable plastic bag. With both the meat and marinade sealed up in the bag, this is a good option for anyone with a small, crowded refrigerator.

Kitchen Timer I can't tell you how many times I think I'm going to time my grilling steak by looking at my watch, and the next thing you know I get to watching *Bonanza* on the television (that's my favorite show) and I lose all track of time. That's why I love my handy kitchen timer. It lets me know when my pork chops are finished grilling, and when my hard-boiled egg is finished. These can be bought in larger supermarkets.

Whisk When you really want to mix it up, a whisk is the way to go. Salad dressings, marinades, and eggs all blend best with a little whisk action. Plus, whisks are one of those great kitchen tools that you can hand off to a toddler to play with. Have a few on hand.

Skewers

Skewers make for instant party atmosphere. When we've got people over to the house, or when we just feel like having a party ourselves, a hand-held appetizer is the Foreman family favorite way to kick off a meal or party. Even the youngest Foremans love them, because the chunks of meat and veggies are the perfect size for little fingers. I like to offer at least two types—it's so easy to assemble skewers ahead of time, refrigerate, and then grill them in minutes as you need them. My kids tell me that skewers are also great party foods for the dorm room. That hot-off-the-grill flavor hits the spot after all the bags of chips and gallons of French onion dip.

Sometimes Sizzling Shrimp and Mango Kebabs • Chicken Satays with Peanut Dipping Sauce • Greek-Style Chicken Kebabs • India Chicken Kebabs • Sirloin Beef Brochettes with Honey-Soy Marinade • Frank-'n-Pineapple Kebabs • Grilled Pork and Grape Kebabs • 1-2-3 Lamb Kebabs

Sometimes Sizzling Shrimp and Mango Kebabs

One of my all-time favorite combinations, and a knockout with the crowd, shrimp and mango kebabs are delicious when they come sizzling off the grill, but they're just as good after the sizzling has stopped. Cold, they're nothing but refreshing, so go ahead and make them ahead of time, refrigerate, and serve them later.

Serves 4

½ cup olive oil

¼ cup sherry vinegar

2 garlic cloves, crushed

1 tablespoon minced fresh ginger

½ teaspoon freshly ground black pepper

1½ pounds shelled and deveined medium shrimp

2 mangoes, cut into big cubes

8 (8-inch) bamboo skewers

1 lemon, cut into 8 wedges

1 Combine the olive oil, vinegar, garlic, ginger, and pepper in a shallow baking dish. Add the shrimp and mango and stir gently to coat. Cover with plastic wrap and refrigerate for at least 30 minutes or up to 2 hours.

2 Preheat the grill to high.

3 Thread the shrimp and mango onto the skewers. Top each with a lemon wedge. Grill the skewers (in batches, if necessary, depending upon the size of your grill) for about 3 minutes, until the shrimp are white and firm to the touch. Serve immediately.

Nutritional values per serving
calories 375; protein 35 g; carbohydrates 21 g; fiber 2 g;
total fat 17 g; saturated fat 3 g; cholesterol 259 mg; sodium 255 mg

QUICK ON A STICK
Foreman's Favorite
Kebab Add-Ons

One of the things I love best about kebabs is that you can make up skewer combinations as you go along. It's easy and lots of fun too, so you can make your own championship-winning skewers depending upon what you've got on hand. These are some of the ingredients that we love to use; cut them into bite-sized pieces before sticking them onto bamboo skewers. Mix and match with the sauces below.

Chicken • Turkey • Pork • Beef • Lamb • Sausages • Ham • Scallops •
Shrimp • Bell Peppers • Eggplant • Zucchini • Fennel •
Cherry Tomatoes • Baby carrots • Pearl onions • Mushrooms •
Radishes • Snow peas • Watermelon • Mango • Pineapple

Peanut Dipping Sauce (page 17) • Ketchup Sauce (page 24) •
Nothing-But-Delicious Sauce (page 110) • Horseradish Cream
(page 130) • Spicy Soy Sauce (page 126) • Chimichurri Sauce (page 138) •
Molasses Barbecue Sauce (page 140) • Creamy Dijon Sauce (page 144) •
Championship Chipotle BBQ Sauce (page 188) • Texas 2-Step Sauce
(page 189) • Ginger Dipping Sauce (page 190) • Simple Garlic
Yogurt Sauce (page 191)

Chicken Satays with Peanut Dipping Sauce

I see these on menus everywhere I go and have found that they're easily prepared at home on the indoor grill. While the grown-ups I know find them delicious and a little exotic, the kids love the peanut butter and gobble these up like mad. Prepare the dipping sauce while the chicken soaks in the flavorful Southeast Asian marinade. You can substitute turkey, pork, or beef for the chicken.

Serves 4

MARINADE

¾ cup canned unsweetened coconut milk

1 teaspoon ground ginger

1 teaspoon curry powder

2 tablespoons fresh lime juice

2 pounds boneless, skinless chicken breasts, pounded to ½-inch thickness, then cut into ½-inch-wide strips

8 (8-inch) bamboo skewers

1 In a medium bowl, whisk together the coconut milk, ginger, curry, and lime juice.

2 Thread the chicken strips onto the skewers, making an "S" shape with each piece of chicken, and lay the skewers in a shallow baking dish. Pour the marinade over, cover, and refrigerate for at least 1 hour or overnight.

PEANUT DIPPING SAUCE

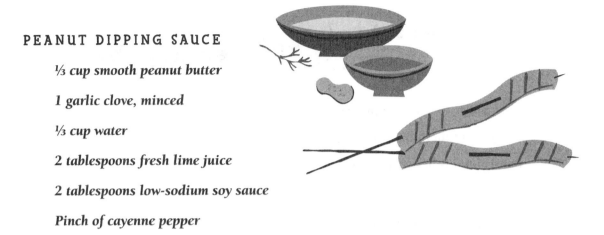

⅓ cup smooth peanut butter

1 garlic clove, minced

⅓ cup water

2 tablespoons fresh lime juice

2 tablespoons low-sodium soy sauce

Pinch of cayenne pepper

In a medium bowl, whisk together until smooth the peanut butter, garlic, water, lime juice, soy sauce, and cayenne. Cover with plastic wrap and keep at room temperature until ready to serve.

TO GRILL

1 Preheat the grill to high.

2 Grill the chicken (in batches, if necessary, depending upon the size of your grill) for about 4 minutes, until it has taken on grill marks and is cooked through. Serve immediately on a tray with a dish of dipping sauce alongside.

Nutritional values per serving

calories 429; protein 60 g; carbohydrates 6 g; fiber 3 g;
total fat 18 g; saturated fat 5 g; cholesterol 132 mg; sodium 287 mg

Greek-Style Chicken Kebabs

These kebabs are my eating philosophy on a stick: fresh, healthy ingredients, perfectly grilled, that can satisfy even a heavyweight-champion-of-the-world appetite like mine!

Serves 4

> *2 tablespoons olive oil*
>
> *Juice of 1 lemon*
>
> *4 garlic cloves, crushed*
>
> *1 teaspoon dried oregano*
>
> *1 teaspoon salt*
>
> *1 teaspoon freshly ground black pepper*
>
> *2 pounds boneless, skinless chicken breasts, cut into 1-inch cubes*
>
> *1 large red onion, cut into 1-inch chunks*
>
> *8 (8-inch) bamboo skewers*

1 In a large bowl, whisk together the olive oil, lemon juice, garlic, oregano, salt, and pepper. Add the chicken and onion and turn to coat. Cover with plastic wrap and marinate in the refrigerator for at least 30 minutes or up to 2 hours.

2 Preheat the grill to high.

3 Thread the chicken and onion onto the skewers, reserving the marinade in the bowl. Grill the skewers (in batches, if necessary, depending upon the size of your grill) for 2 minutes and then brush with the reserved marinade; discard any remaining marinade. Grill for about 2 minutes more, until the chicken has taken on grill marks and is cooked through. Serve immediately.

Nutritional values per serving
calories 333; protein 53 g; carbohydrates 5 g; fiber 1 g;
total fat 10 g; saturated fat 2 g; cholesterol 132 mg; sodium 619 mg

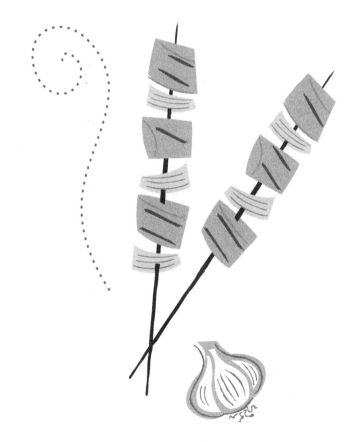

India Chicken Kebabs

As a little kid growing up in the roughest part of Houston, I never imagined that I would travel the world many, many times over, but I have. In between running for planes and climbing into cars, I eat. I love spices and always reach first for anything Indian. Those folks know spice! The chicken should marinate for at least 2 hours, so plan ahead.

Serves 4

¼ cup low-fat plain yogurt

Juice of 1 lemon

4 garlic cloves, minced

½ teaspoon ground cumin

½ teaspoon ground coriander

¼ teaspoon ground ginger

¼ teaspoon red pepper flakes

½ teaspoon salt

2 pounds boneless, skinless chicken breasts, cut into 1-inch cubes

8 (8-inch) bamboo skewers

1 In a medium bowl, stir together the yogurt, lemon juice, garlic, cumin, coriander, ginger, red pepper flakes, and salt. Add the chicken and stir to coat. Cover with plastic wrap and refrigerate for at least 2 hours or overnight.

2 Preheat the grill to high and spray with nonstick cooking spray.

3 Thread the chicken pieces onto the skewers. Grill the kebabs (in batches, if necessary, depending upon the size of your grill) for about 4 minutes, until they have taken on grill marks and are cooked through. Serve immediately.

Nutritional values per serving

calories 270; protein 53 g; carbohydrates 4 g; fiber 0 g;
total fat 3 g; saturated fat 1 g; cholesterol 132 mg; sodium 393 mg

Sirloin Beef Brochettes with Honey-Soy Marinade

In our family, I'm the grill master when it comes to beef; each of my ten kids has a special way they like their steaks and I know them all! These crowd-pleasing sirloin skewers have a slight sweetness and the strong scent of cilantro. The small chunks of meat take minutes on the grill and make perfect finger food for kids or adults. To turn this into a main course salad, slide the beef chunks off the skewers and serve over mixed greens.

Serves 4

MARINADE

⅓ cup olive oil

2 garlic cloves, minced

1 jalapeño pepper, minced

2 tablespoons low-sodium soy sauce

1 tablespoon honey

¾ cup chopped fresh cilantro leaves

2 pounds boneless sirloin steak, cut into 1-inch cubes

Whisk together the olive oil, garlic, jalapeño, soy sauce, and honey in a shallow baking dish. Add the cilantro leaves and whisk again. Add the beef cubes to the marinade and turn to coat. Cover with plastic wrap and refrigerate for at least 2 hours or overnight.

TO GRILL

8 (8-inch) bamboo skewers

½ teaspoon salt

½ teaspoon freshly ground black pepper

1 Preheat the grill to high.

2 Thread the beef onto the skewers and season with the salt and pepper. Grill the skewers (in batches, if necessary, depending upon the size of your grill) for about 3 minutes, until the beef is browned on the outside but still pink in the center. Serve immediately.

Nutritional values per serving
calories 588; protein 45 g; carbohydrates 3 g; fiber .5 g;
total fat 43 g; saturated fat 15 g; cholesterol 150 mg; sodium 498 mg

Frank-'n-Pineapple Kebabs

I don't think I've ever met a kid who didn't want to help out in the kitchen. Kids love to announce "I made it" when putting out snacks or lunch for their friends. These skewers have seen our family through countless sleepovers and after-school snack sessions. This is a perfect I-did-it-myself dish, suitable for seven- or eight-year-olds under the watchful eyes of their parents. And don't forget to address the young chef as "Dr. Frank-'n-Pineapple, I Presume."

Serves 4 hungry kids

KETCHUP SAUCE

½ cup ketchup

1 tablespoon mustard

1 tablespoon light brown sugar

In a small serving bowl, stir together the ketchup, mustard, and brown sugar until smooth. Set aside 2 tablespoons to be used as a glaze for the skewers and reserve the rest to serve as a dipping sauce.

HOT DOGS

4 turkey or chicken hot dogs, preferably organic

2 slices pineapple (each 1 inch thick), fresh or canned, cored

8 (8-inch) bamboo skewers

1 Preheat the grill to medium.

2 Cut the hot dogs into 2-inch segments. Cut each pineapple slice into 8 wedges. Thread the pieces onto the skewers, alternating the hot dog and the pineapple. Brush the kebabs lightly with the 2 tablespoons sauce and then grill (in batches, if necessary, depending upon the size of your grill) for about 4 minutes, until the hot dogs are hot throughout and thoroughly cooked. Serve immediately with the reserved ketchup sauce on the side.

Nutritional values per serving
calories 173; protein 7 g; carbohydrates 18 g; fiber 1 g;
total fat 8 g; saturated fat 3 g; cholesterol 48 mg; sodium 1,110 mg

Grilled Pork and Grape Kebabs

Grapes not only look great as part of a kebab, but they taste great grilled. I'm always looking for ways to incorporate fruits and vegetables into everything I and my family eat, and skewers are a perfect opportunity. Make Spicy Spanish Rub or buy one of the commercially prepared spice rubs. I like rubs that pack power—if you're buying spice rub, check the label for ingredients like cayenne pepper, chiles, and garlic.

Serves 4

> *3 tablespoons orange juice*
>
> *2 tablespoons olive oil*
>
> *1 garlic clove, minced*
>
> *2 pounds pork tenderloin, cut into 1-inch cubes*
>
> *½ pound large green seedless grapes*
>
> *8 (8-inch) bamboo skewers*
>
> *Spicy Spanish Rub (page 192)*

1 In a small bowl, combine the orange juice, olive oil, and garlic.

2 Thread the cubes of pork and the grapes, alternately, onto the skewers. Lay the skewers in a shallow baking dish and sprinkle with the rub. Pour the olive oil mixture over and turn the skewers to coat. Cover with plastic wrap and refrigerate for at least 1 hour or overnight.

3 Preheat the grill to high.

4 Grill the kebabs (in batches, if necessary, depending upon the size of your grill) for about 4 minutes, until they take on grill marks and feel firm to the touch. Serve hot or at room temperature.

Nutritional values per serving
calories 382; protein 48 g; carbohydrates 12 g; fiber 1 g;
total fat 15 g; saturated fat 4 g; cholesterol 147 mg; sodium 115 mg

1-2-3 Lamb Kebabs

Many folks say they don't care for lamb, but when I ask 'em why, they usually admit that they just never ate it growing up. Well, as soon as my kids are about as high as my knee, I feed 'em little chunks of lamb, and POW!, another lamb-lover is born. I love lamb and I think you will too. We serve these kebabs at family gatherings with Simple Garlic Yogurt Sauce (page 191). These get marinated overnight and they're as simple as 1-2-3.

Serves 4

½ cup red wine vinegar

½ cup olive oil

2 tablespoons low-sodium soy sauce

½ teaspoon dried thyme

½ teaspoon dried oregano

2 pounds lamb (from the leg or the loin), cut into 1-inch cubes

1 pint cherry tomatoes

4 small yellow onions, quartered

8 (8-inch) bamboo skewers

1 In a small bowl, whisk together the vinegar, olive oil, soy sauce, and dried herbs.

2 Thread the lamb, cherry tomatoes, and onion sections onto the skewers, alternating as you like. Lay the lamb skewers in a shallow baking dish. Whisk the marinade again, and then pour over the skewers. Refrigerate overnight.

3 Preheat the grill to high.

4 Grill the skewers (in batches, if necessary, depending upon the size of your grill) for about 3 minutes, until the lamb is browned on the outside but still pink in the center and the vegetables are soft and charred.

Nutritional values per serving
calories 412; protein 48 g; carbohydrates 10 g; fiber 2 g;
total fat 19 g; saturated fat 5 g; cholesterol 150 mg; sodium 244 mg

Quesadillas and Tacos

On the days when I've got a house full of kids—after practice or swimming in the pool—quesadillas and tacos are the way to go. I'll help the kids set up an assembly line of ingredients and they can just go to it, making one after another, filling them as they like. Even on days when we're outside around the pool, I'll still set up the indoor grill—this way I don't worry about the kids being around hot coals. I put in my order with the head chef of the moment, jump in the pool cannonball style, and come out to a freshly grilled quesadilla.

Flaming Red Pepper Shrimp Quesadillas • Cheddar Quesadillas with Cherry Tomatoes • Chicken Quesadillas • 'Dia Dogs • Big Tex Tacos • Mahi Tacos Adobo with Avocado Salsa

31

Flaming Red Pepper Shrimp Quesadillas

My son George III (we call him Monk, but he'll have to tell you why) is the Quesadilla King in our house—he can always transform tortillas and whatever we have in the fridge into something outstanding. Monk makes these quesadillas with a spicy pepper Jack and fresh shrimp. When it comes to fresh guacamole (page 180), I'm the champ and I'll always whip up a double batch to spoon over his quesadilla creations.

Makes 4 quesadillas; serves 4

> *½ pound shelled and deveined small shrimp*
>
> *5 tablespoons olive oil*
>
> *1 garlic clove, minced*
>
> *½ teaspoon red pepper flakes*
>
> *2 red bell peppers*
>
> *Salt and freshly ground black pepper*
>
> *8 (8-inch) flour tortillas*
>
> *4 ounces shredded pepper Jack cheese (1 cup)*

1 Rinse the shrimp, pat dry with paper towels, and transfer to a medium bowl. Add 3 tablespoons of the olive oil, the garlic, and red pepper flakes. Cover with plastic wrap and refrigerate for 30 minutes.

2 Preheat the grill to high.

3 While the shrimp are marinating, quarter, core, and seed the bell peppers. Put the peppers in a shallow bowl and toss with the remaining 2 tablespoons olive oil to coat. Sprinkle with salt and pepper. Lay the bell pepper quarters on the grill and cook for 6 minutes, until they are soft and charred. Transfer to a paper-towel-lined plate to cool; keep the grill on high. When the peppers are cool enough to handle, slice into thin matchsticks.

4 Grill the shrimp for 3 minutes, until opaque and firm to the touch. Transfer to a plate. Wipe the grill with a damp paper towel to clear away any charred bits; keep the grill on high.

5 Lay 4 of the tortillas on a clean work surface and sprinkle 3 tablespoons of the shredded cheese over each of them. Divide the shrimp and bell pepper slivers on top. Sprinkle the remaining cheese over the quesadillas, then top with the remaining 4 tortillas.

6 Use a spatula to transfer the quesadillas to the grill, cooking 1 or 2 at a time, depending upon the size of your grill. Cook the quesadillas for about 3 minutes, until the cheese has completely melted. Transfer the quesadillas to a cutting board. Cut each quesadilla into 4 pieces and serve immediately.

Nutritional values per serving
calories 646; protein 27 g; carbohydrates 59 g; fiber 4 g;
total fat 35 g; saturated fat 9 g; cholesterol 116 mg; sodium 744 mg

Cheddar Quesadillas with Cherry Tomatoes

I think of this as a getting-close-to-the-border grilled cheese. Melted cheddar and tomatoes get a little zing from balsamic vinegar. Cherry tomatoes stay fresh in the refrigerator for over a week, so they're handy to keep around. Spoon some store-bought salsa over the top of this quesadilla and maybe a little light sour cream.

Makes 4 quesadillas; serves 4

> *1 cup cherry tomatoes, thinly sliced*
>
> *1 tablespoon balsamic vinegar*
>
> *¼ teaspoon salt*
>
> *8 (8-inch) flour tortillas*
>
> *4 ounces shredded sharp cheddar cheese (1 cup)*
>
> *½ small red onion, finely chopped*

1 In a medium bowl, combine the tomatoes, vinegar, and salt.

2 Lay 4 of the tortillas on a clean work surface. Sprinkle half of the shredded cheese over the tortillas. Spoon the tomato slices and their juice over the shredded cheese, followed by the onion. Finish by sprinkling the remaining cheese on top and covering with the remaining 4 tortillas.

3 Preheat the grill to high.

4 Use a spatula to transfer the quesadillas to the grill, cooking 1 or 2 at a time, depending upon the size of your grill. Cook for about 3 minutes, until the cheese has completely melted. Transfer the quesadillas to a cutting board. Cut each quesadilla into 4 pieces and serve immediately.

Nutritional values per serving
calories 385; protein 12 g; carbohydrates 58 g; fiber 4 g;
total fat 11 g; saturated fat 5 g; cholesterol 15 mg; sodium 676 mg

Chicken Quesadillas

This is an easy, nobody-doesn't-love-'em Mexican classic, a staple of snackers everywhere. When the kids have their friends over, I'll set up an assembly line of all the ingredients. I grill the chicken beforehand and either refrigerate or keep at room temperature until needed. And then I just keep them coming . . . as fast as I can.

Makes 4 quesadillas; serves 4

⅓ cup fresh lime juice (from 4 limes)

2 tablespoons olive oil

2 teaspoons dried oregano

½ teaspoon salt

½ teaspoon freshly ground black pepper

2 or 3 drops hot sauce

1½ pounds boneless, skinless chicken breasts, pounded to ½-inch thickness, then cut into 1-inch-wide strips

8 (8-inch) flour tortillas

½ cup store-bought salsa

4 ounces shredded pepper Jack cheese (1 cup)

¼ cup chopped fresh cilantro leaves

1 In a shallow baking dish, whisk together the lime juice, olive oil, oregano, salt, pepper, and hot sauce. Add the chicken strips and toss gently to combine. Cover and refrigerate for at least 30 minutes or overnight.

2 Preheat the grill to high.

3 Grill the chicken pieces for 3 minutes, until they have taken on grill marks and are cooked through. Transfer the chicken to a plate; keep the grill on high.

4 Lay 4 of the tortillas on a clean work surface and spread 1 tablespoon of the salsa over each. Divide the chicken among the tortillas and top with a liberal sprinkling of the cheese and then the cilantro leaves. Cover with the remaining 4 tortillas.

5 Use a spatula to transfer the quesadillas to the grill, cooking 1 or 2 at a time, depending upon the size of your grill. Cook for about 3 minutes, until the cheese has completely melted. Transfer the quesadillas to a cutting board. Cut each quesadilla into 4 pieces and serve immediately, topped with the remaining salsa.

Nutritional values per serving
calories 689; protein 56 g; carbohydrates 58 g; fiber 4 g;
total fat 26 g; saturated fat 9 g; cholesterol 129 mg; sodium 1,108 mg

'Dia Dogs

'Dia as in quesadilla, 'dia as in the kids could eat them all day long. Any hot dogs will do, but we're huge fans of the organic beef, chicken, or turkey dogs available now. Not only do they taste better, but we know that they contain good wholesome stuff. If serving these to toddlers, don't forget to cut the hot dogs into bite-sized pieces before rolling them in the tortillas to make them easier to eat.

Serves 4

> *4 hot dogs, preferably organic*
>
> *4 (10-inch) flour tortillas*
>
> *¼ cup sweet pickle relish*
>
> *4 ounces shredded Monterey Jack or cheddar cheese (1 cup)*

1 Preheat the grill to high.

2 Split the hot dogs in half lengthwise. Grill for 3 minutes, until well browned.

3 While the hot dogs are grilling, spread each tortilla with 1 tablespoon relish and sprinkle with ¼ cup cheese. Cut the tortillas in half.

4 Tightly roll each grilled hot dog half in a tortilla half. Grill (in batches, if necessary, depending upon the size of your grill) until the cheese melts and the tortillas are browned, about 1 minute. Serve immediately.

Nutritional values per serving
calories 543; protein 20 g; carbohydrates 47 g; fiber 3 g;
total fat 30 g; saturated fat 8 g; cholesterol 60 mg; sodium 1,201 mg

MY KNOCKOUT POOL-PARTY TACOS

We set up a long table, everything to be grilled on one side, the grill in the middle (with a cutting board next to it for slicing meat and fish into strips), and all the fixin's for the finished tacos on the other side. Gallons of iced tea and cold lemonade are at the end of the buffet table.

Flour tortillas • Hard taco shells • Grilled shrimp •
Grilled boneless, skinless chicken breasts • Grilled flank steak •
Grilled mahi-mahi • Cooked bacon, crumbled into bits •
Shredded Monterey Jack cheese • Shredded cheddar cheese •
Grilled red bell peppers • Grilled asparagus • Cooked corn kernels
• Sliced cherry tomatoes • Diced red onion • Shredded lettuce •
Diced mango • Chopped fresh cilantro leaves • Salsa • Guacamole •
Light sour cream • Lime wedges

Big Tex Tacos

I n my home state of Texas, we love steak and we love the food of Mexico. These tacos satisfy hungry steak-lovers like the Foremans. The steak takes only a few minutes to cook, and then the slices are tucked with the other ingredients into a spicy fresh-flavored taco. There's little waiting and even less cooking involved in this fast supper or lunch.

Makes 8 tacos; serves 4

1½ pounds strip steak, about 1 inch thick

1 tablespoon olive oil

Brown Sugar Spice Rub (page 193)

8 (8-inch) flour tortillas

¼ head iceberg lettuce, shredded

1 cup Simple Guacamole (page 180, or store bought)

1 cup store-bought salsa

1 lime, cut into 8 wedges

1 Preheat the grill to high.

2 Rub the steak with the olive oil and then with the spice rub. Grill the steak for 5 minutes for medium-rare. It should have grill marks and feel fairly firm to the touch. Transfer the steak to a cutting board and let it rest for 5 minutes; keep the grill on but turn to low.

3 Warm the tortillas on the grill, leaving the top up, while you slice the steak. Cut the meat into thin slices across the grain.

4 Fill each tortilla with a couple of slices of steak, some shredded lettuce, a spoonful each of guacamole and salsa, and a squirt of lime juice. Or just bring everything to the table and let folks dig in and make their own.

Nutritional values per serving
calories 772; protein 50 g; carbohydrates 66 g; fiber 9 g;
total fat 37 g; saturated fat 8 g; cholesterol 100 mg; sodium 1,262 mg

Mahi Tacos Adobo with Avocado Salsa

Adobo spice mix is available in most grocery stores and gives fish a real jab of Latin flavor. Mahi-mahi is one of the best fish for indoor grilling— it has firm moist flesh with great flavor all on its own, and holds together nicely for salads or sandwiches. While it's sometimes referred to as dolphinfish, tell the kids that mahi-mahi isn't related to Flipper at all . . . in fact, I don't think they've ever met. We prefer soft tacos (they haven't been fried), but you could easily substitute the crisp type. The avocado salsa is championship material, so we make extra to spoon onto burgers or serve with chips.

Makes 8 tacos; serves 4

AVOCADO SALSA

2 avocados, halved, pitted, and cut into chunks

1 cup diced mango

1 cup diced pineapple

1 small red onion, diced

1 jalapeño pepper, halved, seeded, and thinly sliced

1 teaspoon salt

½ teaspoon freshly ground black pepper

¼ cup chopped fresh cilantro leaves

Juice of 1 lime

Mix together all of the ingredients in a medium bowl. As with guacamole, the salsa shouldn't be made more than a couple of hours in advance or the avocado will start to discolor. Cover with plastic wrap and keep at room temperature until ready to serve.

TACOS

4 (6-ounce) skinless mahi-mahi fillets, about 1 inch thick

2 tablespoons adobo spice mix

½ lime

8 (8-inch) flour tortillas

½ head iceberg lettuce, shredded

1 Rub both sides of the fish fillets with the adobo.

2 Preheat the grill to high and then spray with nonstick cooking spray.

3 Grill the fish (in batches, if necessary, depending upon the size of your grill) for 4 minutes. To test for doneness, prod an edge of the fillet with a fork. The fish should flake easily. Transfer the cooked fillets to a plate; keep the grill on but turn to low. Cut the fillets into ½-inch strips. Squeeze the lime over the fish.

4 Warm the tortillas on the grill, leaving the top up. Fill each tortilla with a few strips of fish, some shredded lettuce, and a few tablespoons of avocado salsa. Serve immediately.

Nutritional values per serving
calories 683; protein 43 g; carbohydrates 77 g; fiber 10 g;
total fat 24 g; saturated fat 4 g; cholesterol 125 mg; sodium 1,580 mg

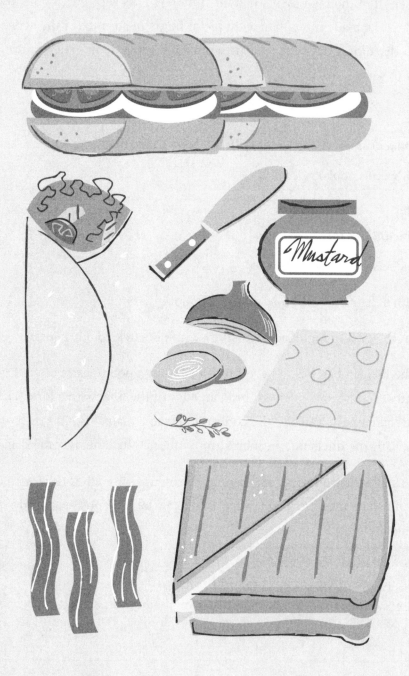

Sandwiches: Grilled, Wrapped, and Otherwise

With ten kids, I've encountered more than most when it comes to special orders. One George won't eat it if it doesn't have melted American on it. Another George wants no cheese at all. One daughter, Natalie, likes grilled mango, while another, Michi, loves mango but wants it fresh. Depending on what we've got in the refrigerator, my best sandwiches are built from a combination of fresh and grilled fillings, depending on who's doing the eating.

Best British Pub Classic Grilled Cheddar • Grilled Provolone, Tomato, and Oregano • Panini with a Pesto Punch • Grilled Fontina with Greens and Tomato • Ham and Cheese Please • Smokin' Turkey Sandwiches • A Cuban Reuben • Rancho Red Pepper Chicken Melts • Open-Faced Portobello-Fontina Melts • Hamburger Wellington • Kid Creole Catfish Po'boys • Chile-Spiked Pork Rolls • Chicken-Caesar Salad Wraps • Fresh Spinach and Gruyère Wraps • Teriyaki Tofu Wraps

WHO GRILLED MY CHEESE?
A Fridge Full of Possibilities

Whenever folks tell me about how they use their Lean Mean Grilling Machine, grilled cheese is often Topic Number One. It's no surprise, since the grill gets the gold medal for the perfect grilled cheese. It cooks both sides of the sandwich at once, and the weight of the top grill makes for a crisp and trim sandwich—golden brown on the outside and cheesy and gooey on the inside—grilled cheese perfection.

Everybody's got their own best way to make one. I've come to admire the Zen-like simplicity of a grilled cheddar, as well as develop a taste for the more exotic examples of this most basic of sandwiches. While grilled cheese isn't exactly what you'd choose if you were trying to become a featherweight, there are options here from indulgent versions to middle-of-the-road ones. And remember—"everything in moderation" works.

If you've got cheese and bread, well then, you've got lunch. Here's how to jazz it up, starting from the outside and making our way toward the center:

Bread: The Foreman family tastes, always a matter of personal preference, run from slim, simple tortillas to big brown slices. From English muffins to yesterday's hamburger buns, all are candidates for gold-medal grilled cheese. Some folks like to butter the outside of their sandwich before grilling for the most golden-brown sandwich. One of my daughters insists on thin, white sandwich bread, with none of the ingredients hanging over the side (she trims everything neatly before tossing the sandwich on the grill). One George serves grilled cheese that he's made on bulky Italian rolls with the tops trimmed off, cutting the rolls down into thin slices that pack big bakery-bread flavor. For the younger kids who are happy eating almost nothing else, I make their grilled cheese on whole grain bread (just to sneak 'em a little nutrition when they aren't looking).

Cheese: I think the most important thing is MELTABILITY! The cheese should go down for the count after the grill cover is closed. Besides American, Swiss, and cheddar there's provolone, Gruyère, fontina, mozzarella. But I have a daughter who prefers a different texture for her grilled cheeses. For her, it's flavor she's looking for, and I've seen her make grilled cheese sandwiches with goat cheese, crumbled blue cheese, and sliced Romano and Parmesan. The sky's the limit!

TEN LITTLE EXTRAS FOR THE GREATEST GRILLED CHEESE

The best sandwiches venture beyond the nuts and bolts of cheese and bread to some great-tasting add-ons. Raid the refrigerator and pile on the flavor.

Bacon: When I'm in the mood to indulge, it's usually bacon I crave. Layer grilled bacon (see page 214) over the cheese before grilling the whole sandwich, and you've got what I call a Diner Classic. I know plenty of folks who think that everything's better with bacon on it. I know this is true when it comes to grilled cheese. (I don't think it's true when it comes to pie, though.)

Lettuce and tomato: Everything's better with a little bit of salad. I dress up a grilled cheese just as I would any other sandwich—but I'll grill the tomato slices first to give them a little extra flavor and make them even juicier. As for lettuce, I love to use all types—red leaf, romaine, and watercress too. And I love raw spinach leaves—they're crisp greens that weigh in heavier on the nutrition scale than regular iceberg.

Chutney and flavored mustards: Whether the crew is craving hot and spicy or a softer, sweet flavor, I've usually got a jarred mustard or chutney in the fridge that will satisfy. With whole grain texture and flavors that run from herbs to horseradish, I keep a few types of mustard on hand just to mix it up, or I'll mix a little honey into a tablespoon of plain old Dijon for a homemade honey mustard. And chutneys add their own special texture to grilled cheese. It's a great way to layer on some heavyweight impact that's as easy as spreading butter on bread.

Fruit and nuts: To make a cheese plate in a sandwich, add chopped walnuts or pecans and thinly sliced pears or apples (or even grapes) before grilling cheddar on brown bread. There's a reason that cheese, nuts, and fruit are always served together: they're delicious.

Fresh herbs: Chop fresh basil, parsley, cilantro, or oregano leaves and add to a sandwich before grilling for unbeatable fresh and flavorful results. A great grown-up grilled cheese.

Grilled onions: Slice and grill yellow or red onions (see page 169) to add bite to any type of cheese. Layer the grilled rings on as heavily or as lightly as you like them.

Tomato sauce: For a grilled English muffin pizza, the kids spoon some tomato sauce onto an English muffin and top with sliced mozzarella. A sprinkling of oregano and onto the grill it goes for a grilled cheese version of what, for many grown-ups, was the first thing they ever made as kids.

Sliced jalapeño: For a 5-alarm grilled cheese, thinly slice some jalapeño onto cheddar or Swiss before grilling. And a dash of hot sauce can really turn up the heat for anyone who wants a fiery grilled cheese.

Garlic: Rub a halved clove of garlic over the outside of golden-brown grilled cheese. The toasted bread will take on the great garlic aroma with just a little bit of the flavor. Folks love this little trick.

Chocolate-hazelnut spread: The last word in grilled cheese contains no cheese at all: spread jarred chocolate-hazelnut spread on white bread and grill until golden brown for the ultimate in grilled dessert sandwiches.

Best British Pub Classic Grilled Cheddar

England makes some of the best cheddar cheeses in the world. If you're feeling like a cheese shop adventure, search out a Cheshire or, from the good ol' U.S. of A., a knockout Vermont Cheddar, but any cheddar will do. Don't skimp on the spicy mustard and pickles, though!

Serves 2

> *4 slices sourdough bread*
>
> *2 tablespoons butter*
>
> *2 tablespoons whole grain mustard*
>
> *6 ounces sharp cheddar cheese, thinly sliced*
>
> *8 bread-and-butter pickle slices*

1 Preheat the grill to medium.

2 Lay the slices of bread on a clean work surface and spread with the butter. Turn over and spread the mustard over 2 of the slices. Cover the other 2 slices with the cheddar. Arrange the pickle slices over the cheddar and then place the other mustard-spread slices on top, butter side up.

3 Grill the sandwiches for about 2 minutes, until the cheese has melted and the bread is golden brown. Cut on the diagonal and serve immediately.

Nutritional values per serving
calories 686; protein 27 g; carbohydrates 44 g; fiber 2 g;
total fat 41 g; saturated fat 25 g; cholesterol 119 mg; sodium 1,783 mg

Grilled Provolone, Tomato, and Oregano

It's funny how a little bit of oregano can take an otherwise regular sandwich and make it memorable, but here's the proof. One of the great things about cooking is that it teaches you that sometimes it's the little details that count most, in the kitchen, in the office, in the ring, and everywhere else.

Serves 4

> *1 (12-inch) baguette*
>
> *2 tablespoons olive oil*
>
> *¼ teaspoon dried oregano*
>
> *¼ teaspoon garlic powder*
>
> *6 ounces provolone cheese, thinly sliced*
>
> *2 beefsteak tomatoes, sliced*
>
> *¼ teaspoon salt*

1 Use a serrated knife to slice off the domed top of the baguette, removing just a half inch or so (either discard, or butter and then toast on the grill, cut into cubes, and toss into a salad). Then slice the baguette in half horizontally.

2 Combine the olive oil, oregano, and garlic powder in a small bowl. Drizzle the mixture over both baguette halves.

3 Preheat the grill to medium.

4 Arrange half the cheese slices over the bottom half of the baguette, followed by the tomato slices. Sprinkle with the salt, then add the remaining provolone. Top with the remaining baguette half.

5 Grill the sandwiches (in batches, if necessary, depending upon the size of your grill) for about 3 minutes, until the cheese melts. Cut the sandwich into 4 pieces and serve immediately.

Nutritional values per serving
calories 404; protein 17 g; carbohydrates 38 g; fiber 3 g;
total fat 21 g; saturated fat 9 g; cholesterol 29 mg; sodium 888 mg

Panini with a Pesto Punch

Panini are the new fashion in grilled cheese and have begun popping up on menus all over the country. This simple one is authentically Italian but easily assembled from American supermarket ingredients. It's worth noting that good-quality bakery bread will turn this already delicious sandwich into a real champ.

Serves 4

> 8 slices rustic bread, or 1 Italian loaf, cut into 4 (4-inch) pieces, and halved
>
> ¼ cup store-bought pesto
>
> 8 ounces mozzarella cheese, preferably fresh, sliced

PESTO An Italian concoction made from pounded basil leaves, olive oil, pine nuts, and Parmesan cheese, pesto can be purchased at most supermarkets in the refrigerated section.

1 Preheat the grill to medium.

2 Lay the slices of bread on a clean work surface and spread with the pesto. Arrange the mozzarella over 4 of the slices. Top with the remaining 4 slices bread.

3 Grill the sandwiches (in batches, if necessary, depending upon the size of your grill) for about 3 minutes, until the cheese melts. Serve immediately.

Nutritional values per serving

calories 398; protein 16 g; carbohydrates 29 g; fiber 2 g; total fat 22 g; saturated fat 1 g; cholesterol 43 mg; sodium 920 mg

Grilled Fontina with Greens and Tomato

Here's another contender for the title "Gold Medal Grilled Cheese." I can find fontina in my local grocery stores here in Houston, so I'll bet you can too. It melts great and is perfect with greens and tomato or baby spinach.

Serves 2

> *6 ounces fontina, thinly sliced*
>
> *4 slices firm white bread*
>
> *1 ripe plum tomato, thinly sliced*
>
> *¼ teaspoon salt*
>
> *1 small bunch arugula*
>
> *1 teaspoon balsamic vinegar*

1 Preheat the grill to medium.

2 Divide the fontina between 2 of the bread slices. Add the tomato slices and sprinkle with the salt. Top with a few arugula leaves and drizzle with the balsamic vinegar. Cover with the remaining bread slices.

3 Grill for about 2 minutes, until the cheese melts and the bread is golden brown. Slice on the diagonal and serve immediately.

Nutritional values per serving
calories 596; protein 30 g; carbohydrates 53 g; fiber 3 g;
total fat 29 g; saturated fat 17 g; cholesterol 99 mg; sodium 1,222 mg

Ham and Cheese Please

While it sounds like an ordinary lunch, this sandwich is the extra-special version, with imported Black Forest ham and Gruyère, another great melter that's easy to find. With a flavor that's similar to Swiss cheese, Gruyère packs an even tastier punch. Use pumpernickel bread to make these sandwiches stand out and, as always, serve them hot off the grill.

Serves 2

4 slices pumpernickel bread

2 tablespoons butter

2 tablespoons whole grain mustard

4 ounces Black Forest ham, thinly sliced

4 ounces Gruyère cheese, thinly sliced

Freshly ground black pepper

1 Preheat the grill to medium.

2 Lay the slices of bread on a clean work surface and spread with the butter. Turn over and spread 2 of the slices with the mustard. Cover these slices with the ham and then top with the sliced cheese and a sprinkling of pepper. Cover with the other bread slices, buttered side up.

3 Grill the sandwiches for about 2 minutes, until the cheese melts. Slice on the diagonal and serve immediately.

Nutritional values per serving
calories 571; protein 33 g; carbohydrates 27 g; fiber 3 g;
total fat 37 g; saturated fat 20 g; cholesterol 124 mg; sodium 1,592 mg

Smokin' Turkey Sandwiches

For those times when I want to pack a little more protein into my grilled sandwiches, I'll whip up these smoked turkey sandwiches, made with the ripest avocado I have. Loaded with antioxidants, avocados are one of the "good fats," adding creamy texture and rich taste. Some of my kids prefer their grilled turkey with a little grilled bacon, so we'll add that too.

Serves 2

> *4 slices pumpernickel or rye bread*
>
> *1 tablespoon Dijon mustard*
>
> *4 ounces smoked turkey, thinly sliced*
>
> *1 ripe avocado, halved, pitted, and sliced*
>
> *2 ounces havarti cheese, thinly sliced*

1 Preheat the grill to medium.

2 Lay the slices of bread on a clean work surface and spread them with the mustard. Divide the turkey, followed by the avocado, and finally the havarti over 2 of the pieces of bread. Cover with the remaining 2 slices.

3 Grill the sandwiches for about 3 minutes, until the cheese melts. Slice on the diagonal and serve immediately.

Nutritional values per serving
calories 309; protein 20 g; carbohydrates 26 g; fiber 3 g;
total fat 13 g; saturated fat 1 g; cholesterol 51 mg; sodium 1,159 mg

A Cuban Reuben

When considering the world's great sandwiches, two names usually top the list: the Cuban, a tasty sandwich of roasted pork, ham, and cheese with pickles, pressed flat on a hot grill, is a favorite among my son Monk and his friends. And then there's the Reuben, named for Reuben's deli in New York City, a monument to rye bread, pastrami, and Russian dressing, and a favorite among older Americans (in other words, my friends). Both have their devoted followings. Both can be counted among the world's greatest sandwiches. Both come together in the Foreman household as an unconventional hybrid that we think bridges the sandwich generation gap. Plus, we just love the name.

Serves 4

1 French baguette or Italian bread, quartered, then sliced in half horizontally

2 tablespoons whole grain mustard

¾ pound corned beef or pastrami, thinly sliced

8 ounces sliced ham (8 slices)

1 cup Creamy Light Coleslaw (page 185) or store-bought, drained in a sieve

16 bread-and-butter pickle slices

8 ounces sliced Swiss cheese (8 slices)

1 Preheat the grill to high.

2 Lay the bread halves on a clean work surface. Spread both top and bottom halves with the mustard. Layer onto the bottom halves in the following order: the corned beef, ham, coleslaw, pickle slices, and cheese. Cover each sandwich with the top halves of the bread.

3 Grill the sandwiches (in batches, if necessary, depending upon the size of your grill) until the cheese melts and the bread has flattened and taken on grill marks, about 2 minutes. Serve immediately.

Nutritional values per serving
calories 626; protein 51 g; carbohydrates 45 g; fiber 2 g;
total fat 25 g; saturated fat 13 g; cholesterol 129 mg; sodium 2,361 mg

Rancho Red Pepper Chicken Melts

This is a grilled cheese that eats like a meal. It's got zippy spice and it's one of my favorites. Tangy Emmenthaler cheese is perfect for melting and has a great taste too. Make this all at once or grill the chicken and peppers ahead of time and refrigerate to build into a sandwich later.

Serves 4

> 2 red bell peppers
>
> 3 tablespoons olive oil
>
> Salt and freshly ground black pepper
>
> 1½ pounds boneless, skinless chicken breasts, pounded to ½-inch thickness
>
> ¼ teaspoon sweet paprika or cayenne pepper
>
> 4 (6-inch) hero rolls
>
> 1 tablespoon light mayonnaise
>
> 1 tablespoon ketchup
>
> 4 ounces grated Emmenthaler or Swiss cheese (1 cup)
>
> ½ teaspoon red pepper flakes

1 Preheat the grill to high.

2 Quarter, core, and seed the bell peppers. Put the peppers in a shallow bowl and toss with 2 tablespoons of the olive oil to coat. Sprinkle with salt and pepper. Lay the bell pepper quarters on the grill and cook for 6 minutes, until they are soft and charred. Transfer to a paper-towel-lined plate to cool; keep the grill on high. When the peppers are cool enough to handle, chop them roughly.

3 Rub the chicken breasts with the remaining tablespoon olive oil and sprinkle with ¼ teaspoon salt and the paprika. Grill the chicken breasts (in batches, if necessary, depending upon the size of your grill) for about 3 minutes, until they have taken on grill marks and are cooked through. Transfer the chicken to a cutting board and cut into 2-inch strips; keep the grill on high.

4 Using a serrated knife, slice off about ½ inch from the top of each roll; discard the tops. Slice the rolls in half horizontally. Lay them on a clean work surface. Mix together the mayonnaise and ketchup and spread over the bottom halves of the rolls. Top with the chicken, followed by the peppers, and then the cheese. Season each sandwich with a few red pepper flakes and then close with the tops of the rolls.

5 Grill the sandwiches (in batches, if necessary, depending upon the size of your grill) for about 3 minutes, until the cheese melts. Serve immediately.

Nutritional values per serving
calories 581; protein 54 g; carbohydrates 36 g; fiber 3 g;
total fat 23 g; saturated fat 7 g; cholesterol 129 mg; sodium 784 mg

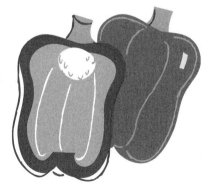

Open-Faced Portobello-Fontina Melts

As an open-faced melt, portobello mushrooms and grated fontina make a terrific start to a bigger dinner, or, with a green salad, the perfect light lunch.

Serves 4

> 1 tablespoon butter, softened
>
> 4 slices white bread
>
> 2 tablespoons olive oil
>
> 2 garlic cloves, minced
>
> 1 tablespoon chopped fresh basil leaves
>
> 4 portobello mushrooms, stemmed
>
> 4 ounces fontina cheese, shredded or thinly sliced
>
> 1 tablespoon chopped fresh parsley leaves

1 Preheat the grill to high.

2 Lightly butter both sides of the bread slices. Grill for 2 minutes, until lightly browned. Transfer to a cutting board or a clean work surface.

3 Combine the olive oil, garlic, and basil in a small bowl. Brush the mushroom caps generously on both sides with the olive oil mixture. Grill the mushrooms (in batches, if necessary, depending upon the size of your grill) for about 4 minutes, until they have dark grill marks and are soft to the touch. Transfer to a cutting board. Keep the grill on but turn to medium and spray with nonstick spray.

4 Slice each mushroom cap into ½-inch-wide strips and arrange over the bread slices. Sprinkle with the fontina and parsley. Transfer the open-faced sandwiches to the grill (in batches, if necessary, depending upon the size of your grill) and lower the top grill for 30 seconds, just to melt the cheese. Serve immediately.

Nutritional values per serving
calories 294; protein 12 g; carbohydrates 19 g; fiber 2 g;
total fat 20 g; saturated fat 8 g; cholesterol 41 mg; sodium 390 mg

Hamburger Wellington

The kids always made fun of "fancy food" when they were little and called everything "Beef Wellington"—beef tenderloin wrapped in puff pastry—no matter what they were eating. I guess they learned about it from television butlers. So we made up our own version and still serve it today. These are more like hamburger panini, so the burgers are meant to be on the thinner side.

Serves 4

> 8 slices white bread
>
> 2 tablespoons butter, softened
>
> 4 slices Swiss cheese (about 4 ounces)
>
> 1 small handful baby spinach
>
> 1 pound ground lean beef
>
> ¼ teaspoon salt
>
> ½ teaspoon freshly ground black pepper

1 Preheat the grill to high.

2 Lay the bread slices on a clean work surface. Lightly butter them and then turn them over. Cover 4 of the slices with a slice of cheese and a few spinach leaves.

3 Form the ground beef into 4 thin patties. Season the patties on both sides with the salt and pepper.

4 Grill the patties (in batches, if necessary, depending upon the size of your grill) for about 3 minutes for medium-rare (or a minute or two longer if you prefer a medium or well-done burger). Put the burgers on top of the spinach—keep the grill on high—and cover with the remaining bread slices, buttered side facing up. Grill the sandwiches until the cheese melts and the bread is golden brown, 30 seconds to 1 minute. Serve immediately—on the good china.

Nutritional values per serving
calories 591; protein 32 g; carbohydrates 26 g; fiber 1 g;
total fat 39 g; saturated fat 18 g; cholesterol 127 mg; sodium 582 mg

Kid Creole Catfish Po'boys

George Jr. loves all things spicy and Cajun, so he gets the name Kid Creole. His lunchtime repertoire includes this famous (in our house, anyway) catfish fillet po'boy, which we think has a lot of star power. As always, using the grill rather than deep-frying means that these po'boys are not fat boys, but they're still a spicy Southern sandwich.

Serves 4

SPICE RUB

2 teaspoons salt

2 teaspoons garlic powder

2 teaspoons sweet paprika

1 teaspoon onion powder

1 teaspoon dried oregano

1 teaspoon freshly ground black pepper

1 teaspoon cayenne pepper

1 teaspoon sugar

Combine all of the ingredients in a jar or plastic bag and shake to mix. (The spice rub can be kept nearly indefinitely but will taste best if used within 1 month. Try it with fish or meat.)

SANDWICHES

½ cup tartar sauce

½ cup sweet pickle relish

4 (6-ounce) skinless catfish fillets

4 (6-inch) hero rolls, halved horizontally

1 Mix together the tartar sauce and the relish in a small bowl. Set aside.

2 Preheat the grill to high and spray with nonstick cooking spray.

3 Rinse the catfish fillets and pat dry with paper towels. Rub both sides of each fillet with the spice mixture. Grill the fillets (in batches, if necessary, depending upon the size of your grill) for about 3 minutes. The fish is done when it is opaque and flakes when poked with a fork. Use a spatula to transfer the cooked fillets to the bottom halves of the rolls. Spoon some of the tartar sauce mixture over the catfish and then cover with the tops of the rolls. Serve immediately.

Nutritional values per serving
calories 525; protein 37 g; carbohydrates 43 g; fiber 2 g;
total fat 24 g; saturated fat 4 g; cholesterol 109 mg; sodium 1,417 mg

Chile-Spiked Pork Rolls

While some sandwiches are a quick fix, piled together in seconds as you stand at the kitchen counter, others are meant to be planned for, organized, and assembled with a little more precision. This is one of those sandwiches—a big hulking masterpiece of pork and Southwestern flavor.

Serves 4

CHILE-SPIKED PORK

3 ounces dried chiles (jalapeños, anchos, or a combination)

3 tablespoons olive oil

3 tablespoons cider vinegar

2 garlic cloves, crushed

1 teaspoon dried oregano

1 teaspoon ground cinnamon

1 whole clove

4 (6-ounce) boneless center-cut pork chops, pounded to ½-inch thickness

Soak the dried chiles in warm water for 15 minutes, until softened; drain. Slice the chiles in half and discard the seeds. Combine the chiles with the olive oil, vinegar, garlic, oregano, cinnamon, and clove in a blender and process until nearly smooth. Pour into a shallow baking dish and add the pork chops, turning to coat. Cover with plastic wrap and refrigerate for at least 2 hours or overnight.

1 small yellow onion, thinly sliced

1 ripe avocado, halved, pitted, and spooned into a bowl

4 hamburger buns

¼ cup chopped fresh cilantro leaves

4 ounces shredded Monterey Jack cheese (1 cup)

1 lime, cut into wedges

1 Preheat the grill to high.

2 Grill the pork (in batches, if necessary, depending upon the size of your grill) for about 3 minutes, until the meat has taken on grill marks and is firm to the touch; keep the grill on high.

3 Grill the onion slices for about 6 minutes, until warm and softened. Transfer the onion slices to the plate along with the cooked chops; keep the grill on high.

4 Spoon some avocado over the bottom halves of the buns and spread it to cover the bread. Add the pork chops and onions and top with the cilantro leaves and cheese. Squeeze some fresh lime juice over each sandwich and close with the top half of the buns. Grill for 30 seconds, just until the cheese melts. Serve immediately.

Nutritional values per serving
calories 610; protein 36 g; carbohydrates 39 g; fiber 8 g;
total fat 36 g; saturated fat 5 g; cholesterol 88 mg; sodium 434 mg

Chicken-Caesar Salad Wraps

I love a big Caesar, right down to the anchovies. This is my version, rolled up in a flour tortilla and ready to travel. It's my favorite wrap to carry out on the terrace when I want to have lunch with my cat, Sonny Liston, who's usually out back napping in the sun.

Serves 4

> 2 pounds boneless, skinless chicken breasts, pounded to ½-inch thickness
>
> 1 tablespoon olive oil
>
> ¼ teaspoon salt
>
> Freshly ground black pepper
>
> ½ cup light mayonnaise
>
> 2 tablespoons Dijon mustard
>
> ½ teaspoon anchovy paste
>
> ½ teaspoon minced garlic
>
> ¼ cup grated Parmesan cheese, preferably freshly grated
>
> 4 romaine lettuce leaves
>
> 4 (10-inch) flour tortillas

1 Preheat the grill to high.

2 Brush the chicken breasts on both sides with the olive oil. Sprinkle with the salt and some pepper. Grill the breasts (in batches, if necessary, depending upon the size of your grill) for about 3 minutes, until they have taken on grill marks and are cooked through. Transfer to a plate and let cool to room temperature. With clean hands, shred the breasts into bite-sized pieces.

3 In a medium bowl, stir together the mayonnaise, mustard, anchovy paste, and garlic. Add the shredded chicken and the Parmesan, season with pepper, and stir to combine. (The salad can be covered and refrigerated overnight at this point.)

4 To assemble the wraps, place a romaine leaf in the center of each tortilla. Top with 1 cup of the chicken mixture. Roll up the wraps, tucking in the bottoms. Serve immediately.

Nutritional values per serving
calories 650; protein 61 g; carbohydrates 44 g; fiber 3 g;
total fat 24 g; saturated fat 6 g; cholesterol 147 mg; sodium 1,025 mg

Fresh Spinach and Gruyère Wraps

This wrap is the direct result of leftovers—my wife had a spinach salad in the refrigerator and I appropriated it for an emergency lunch with a little shredded Gruyère. It's since become a mainstay in the Foreman household, where it is loved by all. If you want to be twelve rounds strong, eat your spinach.

Serves 4

2 teaspoons red wine vinegar

1 teaspoon Dijon mustard

¼ teaspoon salt

¼ teaspoon freshly ground black pepper

2 tablespoons olive oil

2 cups baby spinach

1 small red onion, finely chopped

4 ounces shredded Gruyère cheese (1 cup)

4 (8-inch) flour tortillas

1 hard-boiled egg, chopped

1 Preheat the grill to high.

2 In a medium bowl, whisk together the vinegar, mustard, salt, and pepper. Whisk in the olive oil. Add the spinach and onion and toss to coat.

3 Sprinkle the cheese over the tortillas and then cover with a handful of the spinach and a bit of chopped egg. Roll up the wraps, tucking in the bottoms. Grill the wraps (in batches, if necessary, depending upon the size of your grill) for about 1 minute, until the cheese melts and the spinach wilts. Serve immediately.

Nutritional values per serving
calories 364; protein 15 g; carbohydrates 30 g; fiber 2 g;
total fat 21 g; saturated fat 8 g; cholesterol 85 mg; sodium 483 mg

Teriyaki Tofu Wraps

I cannot tell a lie: I'm not much of a tofu man. But some of my kids went out into the world and took up tofu eating. I appreciate how easy it is to use, and it is a great source of protein. But for me, I say, Where's the beef?

Serves 4

4 (8-inch) flour tortillas

1 cup shredded Napa cabbage or iceberg lettuce

2 scallions, chopped

¼ teaspoon salt

¼ teaspoon freshly ground black pepper

¼ cup teriyaki sauce

2 tablespoons Asian sesame oil

1 tablespoon honey

1 pound extra-firm tofu, drained

1 Lay out the tortillas on a clean work surface. Cover the tortillas with an even layer of cabbage and scallions. Sprinkle with the salt and pepper.

2 Whisk together the teriyaki sauce, sesame oil, and honey in a small bowl.

3 Preheat the grill to medium.

4 On a cutting board, cut the tofu into 6 slabs, each approximately ½ inch thick. Pat dry with paper towels. Brush both sides of each piece of tofu with some of the teriyaki mixture. Grill (in batches, if necessary, depending upon the size of your grill) for 2 minutes. Brush a little more teriyaki mixture on top of each piece of tofu and grill for 2 minutes more. Use a spatula to transfer the cooked tofu to a cutting board. Cut each piece in half.

5 Place 3 pieces of tofu on each of the tortillas. Drizzle some of the remaining teriyaki sauce on top, then roll up the wraps, tucking in the bottoms. Serve immediately.

Nutritional values per serving
calories 374; protein 16 g; carbohydrates 38 g; fiber 2 g;
total fat 17 g; saturated fat 3 g; cholesterol 0 mg; sodium 974 mg

BEST SANDWICH PILE-ONS

Fruit—Whether you grill it first before piling it on, or slice it fresh, apples, pears, avocado, and mango taste great with grilled chicken, sliced turkey, or cheese. Besides adding fiber, color, and crispness, sliced fruit on a sandwich is just plain cheerful.

Grilled vegetables—Grilled eggplant, red bell peppers, thick-sliced onions, or portobello mushrooms turn any sandwich into a big-man meal. Grill the vegetables ahead of time, drizzle them with a little olive oil, and keep in the fridge until needed.

Cheese from everywhere—Besides good old American and cheddar, try a goat or mozzarella, slices from a big hunk of Italian Parmesan, or crumbled Greek feta. Slide any sandwich onto a hot grill to warm and melt the cheese and you've got a sandwich success on your hands.

Out of a jar—Pitted olives, hot peppers, a dash of hot sauce, or flavored mustards add an unexpected kick to even the most ordinary sandwich. Light mayonnaise that I doctor with fresh chopped herbs (basil, tarragon, or cilantro) makes for a green garden-fresh flavor.

From the spice rack—Dried oregano, a pinch of cayenne, or dried parsley sprinkled over a sandwich just before grilling lets everyone know that you care about the little things. Even sandwiches should get the classic combination of salt and pepper. I like the taste of kosher salt best of all. It's what I use in all of my recipes because it has a milder taste than iodized salt and the larger crystals add good texture to food. Sold in large boxes, it's easy to reach in with your fingers or a measuring spoon. And when it comes to pepper, the just-ground taste and aroma that you get with a pepper mill is my favorite.

Burgers

Entire books can be written about burgers (and have been). I've seen folks argue about the kind of meat, the type of bun, if lettuce and tomato are better than onion, and if an everything-on-it is going too far. But there's one thing that most folks agree on—that burgers are a best-of-America kind of meal. And truly great burgers can be made on an indoor grill.

For me, the best burger is made from beef, but these days great burgers are made from ground turkey, lamb, or even fish (or bison or venison, if that's your thing).

I'm the burger meister in our family. Though everyone tries to capture the title, I'm winner and still champ, and I love eating the competition.

The Big George • Aisle 6 Beef Burgers • Chipotle Burgers with Avocado • Brunch Burgers • 3 P's Turkey Burger • Big Cheese Turkey Burger • Spiced Lamb Burgers • Tuna "Sushi" Burgers with Wasabi Mayonnaise

The Big George

For almost everyone who uses any kind of grill, burgers are a main event. Besides the fact that grilling is, hands down, the best way to cook one, burgers are a Top 3 Favorite of every meat-eater I know. For all their simple appeal, burgers require a little finesse, and maybe even a philosophy; here's mine:

Use freshly ground beef with a little fat, which adds flavor. This means lean rather than extra-lean meat (remember, the excess fat will drip off, thanks to the fat-reducing design of the grill). Pre-formed burgers are convenient, but I prefer to make my own, seasoned as I like. Keep in mind that a uniform burger size makes for a uniform cooking time. I believe in moderate portion sizes, so when I'm making 4 burgers I use 1¼ pounds of meat to make 4 patties that weigh about 5 ounces each and are about 1 inch thick. Because I love to pile on the fixin's, I like a burger that's not too thick, with a well-proportioned burger-to-bun ratio. Even with my big and tall appetite, this is more than satisfying—exactly what a hamburger is supposed to be.

TOASTING BUNS on the GRILL

If you've got a grill with the great bun warmer feature, use it. If you don't, preheat the grill to high, lightly butter the inside of the bun (or brush lightly with olive oil) and grill, facedown, for about 2 minutes, until the interior of the bun is golden brown. Bagels are also great toasted on the grill, but I prefer to toast them dry and then spread them with a little butter or cream cheese.

Buns matter, big time. While I usually keep my bread intake to a minimum, hamburger buns are an integral part of a best burger experience and therefore too good to skip. One of my daughters compromises by eating her burgers with a knife and fork, bottom bun only—this is a great way to indulge but still cut calories. As a family we're divided; I love the good ol' American hamburger bun, while the rest of the family have their own favorites: English muffins, brioche rolls from the bakery, or seeded rolls from the deli. But we all agree that toasted buns are best. (See box on page 76.)

Everyone cheers for cheeseburgers, and our favorites include cheddar, Swiss, and fontina. Melting cheese on the grill is fast and easy, but remember to spray the grill with nonstick spray first so that cleanup is also fast and easy.

Serves 4

1¼ pounds lean ground beef

½ teaspoon salt

½ teaspoon freshly ground black pepper

Seasoning of your choice (such as a dash of Worcestershire or hot sauce, or 1 teaspoon Spicy Spanish Rub [page 192] or other spice rub)

4 slices cheese such as American, cheddar, or Swiss (about 4 ounces), or ¼ cup crumbled blue or goat cheese

4 toasted buns (see box on previous page)

4 beefsteak tomato slices

4 leaves romaine lettuce

(continued)

1 Preheat the grill to high and spray with nonstick spray.

2 Put the beef in a medium bowl and add the salt, pepper, and your preferred seasonings. Using a fork, mix the seasonings into the meat and then, with your hands, form the mixture into 4 patties, each about 1 inch thick.

3 Grill the patties (in batches, if necessary, depending upon the size of your grill) for about 3 minutes for medium-rare (or a minute or two longer if you prefer a medium or well-done burger). A medium-rare burger will be browned, with grill marks, but still feel slightly soft when poked. A medium burger will feel a bit firmer, and a well-done burger will be absolutely firm to the touch. When in doubt, just cut into one of the burgers and check inside to make sure it's cooked how you like it. Lay the cheese over the burgers and lower the grill. Grill for 30 seconds, just until the cheese melts.

4 Set the burgers onto the bottom halves of the buns, add a slice of tomato and a leaf of lettuce to each burger, and cover with the tops of the buns. Serve immediately.

Nutritional values per serving
calories 510; protein 36 g; carbohydrates 23 g; fiber 1 g;
total fat 30 g; saturated fat 14 g; cholesterol 112 mg; sodium 697 mg

MAKE IT AND TAKE IT
The Top 10 Travelers

Sometimes leftovers are in such high demand that I'll double up on a recipe just so we've got lunch ready to roll the next day. Resealable disposable containers pack it all up neatly, ready to go into the office refrigerator. These are some of my family's favorites to take on the road:

Chicken Curry Salad (page 114) rolled in flour tortillas to make wraps •
Do-Anything Lemon Chicken Breasts (page 106) over mixed greens •
Montego Bay Jerk Chicken (page 116) with a side order of **Creamy Light Coleslaw** (page 185) • **Spicy Soy Flank Steak** (page 126) in pitas with lettuce and tomato • **Cold Soba with Beef and Cucumber** (page 132) •
Pork Tenderloin with Cucumber-Cashew Salad (page 136) •
Sometimes Sizzling Shrimp and Mango Kebabs (page 14)
over salad greens • **Summer Shrimp Salad** (page 150) • **Simple Grilled Swordfish** (page 154) with **Cherry Tomato Salad** (page 184) •
Nice Tuna Steaks (page 160)

Aisle 6 Beef Burgers

These got their name when I asked my son George III what exactly made his hamburgers so special. "I use everything in aisle 6," he said, referring to the condiment section of our supermarket. And while teriyaki sauce and Parmesan cheese don't seem like natural partners, the result of this everything-but-the-kitchen-sink approach is a knockout.

Serves 4

1¼ pounds lean ground beef

1 small onion, minced

¼ cup teriyaki sauce

3 tablespoons Italian-flavored bread crumbs

2 tablespoons grated Parmesan cheese

1 teaspoon salt

1 teaspoon freshly ground black pepper

3 tablespoons sweet pickle relish

4 Kaiser rolls, toasted (see page 76)

1 Preheat the grill to high and spray with nonstick spray.

2 Put the beef in a medium bowl and add the onion, teriyaki sauce, bread crumbs, Parmesan cheese, salt, and pepper. Using a fork, mix the seasonings into the meat and then form the mixture into 4 patties, each about 1 inch thick.

3 Grill the patties (in batches, if necessary, depending upon the size of your grill) for about 3 minutes for medium-rare (or a minute or two longer if you prefer a medium or well-done burger). Top each burger with a spoonful of sweet pickle relish before sandwiching between a bun. Serve immediately.

Nutritional values per serving
calories 519; protein 33g; carbohydrates 43 g; fiber 2 g;
total fat 23 g; saturated fat 8 g; cholesterol 84 mg; sodium 1,387 mg

Chipotle Burgers with Avocado

From time to time, I pick up a few cans of chipotle chiles in adobo sauce at the supermarket and keep them in the cupboard. I'll add pureed chipotles to grilled sandwiches or quesadillas or spoon some into light sour cream for an instant dip. I love the smoky heat. When I'm in the mood for a spicy burger, this is the one.

Serves 4

- 1¼ *pounds lean ground beef*
- 2 *tablespoons chipotle puree*
- ½ *teaspoon salt*
- ¼ *teaspoon freshly ground black pepper*
- 4 *slices cheddar cheese (about 4 ounces)*
- 1 *avocado, halved, pitted, and sliced*
- ¼ *head iceberg lettuce, shredded*
- 4 *hamburger buns, toasted (see page 76)*

1 Preheat the grill to high and spray with nonstick cooking spray.

2 Put the beef in a medium bowl and add the chipotle puree, salt, and pepper. Using a fork, mix the seasonings into the meat and then, with your hands, form the mixture into 4 patties, each about 1 inch thick.

3 Grill the patties (in batches, if necessary, depending upon the size of your grill) for about 3 minutes for medium-rare (or a minute or two longer if you prefer a medium or well-done burger) before topping each burger with a slice of cheese. Close the grill and cook for 1 minute more, until the cheese melts. Top each burger with a few slices of avocado and some shredded lettuce before sandwiching between a bun.

Nutritional values per serving

calories 590; protein 37 g; carbohydrates 26 g; fiber 3 g;
total fat 38 g; saturated fat 15 g; cholesterol 112 mg; sodium 770 mg

CHIPOTLE PUREE Put canned chipotles and their liquid in a blender or food processor and process until smooth. The puree can be covered with plastic wrap and refrigerated for up to 2 weeks. This stuff is hot-hot-hot, so a little goes a long way. I use it in meat marinades and dips. The puree is sold in some grocery stores, in ethnic markets, or online at ethnicgrocer.com.

Brunch Burgers

Burgers for brunch? Why not! The trademark flavors of the popular brunch cocktail Bloody Mary are here with all the kick and zing you'd expect (but none of the alcohol). Celery salt is key, so don't skip it!

Serves 4

> ¼ cup light sour cream
>
> 5 tablespoons prepared white horseradish
>
> ¼ teaspoon salt
>
> 1¼ pounds lean ground beef
>
> ¼ cup tomato sauce
>
> 2 tablespoons Worcestershire sauce
>
> A dash or 2 of hot sauce
>
> 1 teaspoon celery salt
>
> 4 beefsteak tomato slices
>
> 4 brioche buns or hamburger buns, toasted (see page 76)
>
> 2 celery stalks, with leafy greens, each cut into 4 pieces

1 Preheat the grill to high.

2 In a small bowl, combine the sour cream, 2 tablespoons of the horseradish, and the salt.

3 Put the beef in a medium bowl and add the remaining 3 tablespoons horseradish, the tomato sauce, the Worcestershire sauce, hot sauce, and celery salt. Using a fork, mix the seasonings into the meat and then, with your hands, form the mixture into 4 patties, each about 1 inch thick.

4 Grill the patties (in batches, if necessary, depending upon the size of your grill) for about 3 minutes for medium-rare (or a minute or two longer if you prefer a medium or well-done burger). Top with a tablespoon of the horseradish sour cream and a tomato slice before sandwiching between a toasted bun. Serve immediately with the celery sticks.

Nutritional values per serving
calories 447; protein 35 g; carbohydrates 31 g; fiber 1 g;
total fat 27 g; saturated fat 8 g; cholesterol 84 mg; sodium 1,152 mg

3 P's Turkey Burger

The 3 P's are: pesto, Parmesan, and pine nuts (those last two give you an extra punch of pesto flavor). And the result is an Italian-inspired turkey burger with a garden-fresh flavor that reminds everyone of summer, no matter what time of year it is. Serve these in pitas, as wraps, or on whole wheat bread.

Serves 4

> *1 pound ground turkey*
>
> *⅓ cup pine nuts or walnut pieces*
>
> *3 tablespoons grated Parmesan cheese*
>
> *2 tablespoons store-bought pesto (or 3 if you're a pesto fanatic)*
>
> *¼ teaspoon salt*
>
> *¼ teaspoon freshly ground black pepper*
>
> *4 whole wheat pitas*
>
> *4 romaine lettuce leaves or 1 small handful arugula*
>
> *½ lemon*

1 Preheat the grill to high.

2 Put the turkey in a medium bowl and add the pine nuts, Parmesan, pesto, salt, and pepper. Using a fork, mix the seasonings into the meat and then, with your hands, form the mixture into 4 patties, each about 1 inch thick.

3 Grill the patties (in batches, if necessary, depending upon the size of your grill) for about 4 minutes, until they have taken on grill marks and are cooked through. Put each burger into a pita with some lettuce and a squeeze of lemon juice. Serve immediately.

Nutritional values per serving

calories 369; protein 28 g; carbohydrates 19 g; fiber 3 g;
total fat 21 g; saturated fat 5 g; cholesterol 94 mg; sodium 502 mg

Big Cheese Turkey Burger

In this case the big cheese is Gruyère and it turns simple turkey burgers into a Foreman family favorite. We gobble these up on English muffins with crisp lettuce and juicy tomato.

Serves 4

4 English muffins

2 tablespoons butter

1¼ pounds ground turkey

2 ounces shredded Gruyère cheese (½ cup)

2 scallions, chopped

¼ cup bread crumbs

¼ cup Dijon mustard

½ teaspoon salt

¼ teaspoon freshly ground black pepper

4 romaine lettuce leaves

4 beefsteak tomato slices

1 Preheat the grill to high.

2 Split and butter both the insides and outsides of the English muffins. Grill for 2 minutes, until golden brown. Set aside; keep the grill on high.

3 Put the turkey in a medium bowl and add the cheese, scallions, bread crumbs, mustard, salt, and pepper. Using a fork, mix the seasonings into the meat and then, with your hands, form the mixture into 4 patties, each about 1 inch thick.

4 Grill the patties (in batches, if necessary, depending upon the size of your grill) for about 4 minutes, until they have taken on grill marks and are cooked through. Sandwich a burger, a leaf of lettuce, and a slice of tomato between each English muffin half. Serve immediately.

Nutritional values per serving
calories 497; protein 35 g; carbohydrates 34 g; fiber 2 g;
total fat 24 g; saturated fat 10 g; cholesterol 143 mg; sodium 808 mg

Spiced Lamb Burgers

Here's more of the lamb I love, perfectly spiced. If you can't find lean ground lamb, ask your butcher (and there should be one in the meat section of larger supermarkets) to grind lamb shoulder for you. The difference between ground lamb shoulder and regular ground lamb is downright astounding: lamb shoulder has roughly half the calories and less than a third of the fat but is still incredibly flavorful.

I serve these burgers in whole wheat pitas with crisp cucumber slices. (Mini lamb burgers make great party snacks—make them about 2 inches wide and grill for 2 minutes.) Simple Garlic Yogurt Sauce is cool and delicious spooned over the top.

Serves 4

> 1¼ pounds lean ground lamb
>
> 1 tablespoon ground cumin
>
> ¼ teaspoon ground cinnamon
>
> ½ teaspoon salt
>
> ½ teaspoon freshly ground black pepper
>
> 4 whole wheat pitas
>
> ½ medium cucumber, peeled and sliced
>
> ½ cup Simple Garlic Yogurt Sauce (page 191)

1 Preheat the grill to high.

2 Put the lamb in a medium bowl with the cumin, cinnamon, salt, and pepper. Using a fork, mix the seasonings into the meat and then, with your hands, form the mixture into 4 patties, each about 1 inch thick.

3 Grill the patties (in batches, if necessary, depending upon the size of your grill) for about 3 minutes for medium-rare (or a minute or two longer if you prefer a medium or well-done burger). Put a burger into each pita, stuff a few cucumber slices in there too, and spoon some of the yogurt sauce over the top. Serve immediately.

Nutritional values per serving

calories 364; protein 36 g; carbohydrates 31 g; fiber 6 g;
total fat 12 g; saturated fat 4 g; cholesterol 97 mg; sodium 662 mg

Tuna "Sushi" Burgers with Wasabi Mayonnaise

Sushi in inspiration only, these cooked burgers are served with wasabi mayonnaise, a tribute to the horseradish-like root. Look for wasabi powder in the spice section of your supermarket. Its energizing effects have been re-created in powder form, at less cost and more convenience.

Serves 4

WASABI MAYONNAISE

> *⅓ cup light mayonnaise*
>
> *1 teaspoon wasabi powder*
>
> *½ teaspoon grated lime zest*

Stir together the mayonnaise, wasabi powder, and lime zest in a small bowl. Cover with plastic wrap and keep in the refrigerator for up to 1 week.

BURGERS

> *1¼ pounds fresh, sushi-quality tuna steaks*
>
> *4 scallions, white part only, chopped*
>
> *½ jalapeño pepper, seeded and minced*
>
> *2 garlic cloves, minced*
>
> *1 tablespoon minced fresh ginger*
>
> *1 tablespoon Asian sesame oil*
>
> *1 teaspoon grated lime zest*
>
> *Cornmeal*
>
> *4 brioche buns or hamburger rolls, toasted (see page 76)*

1 On a cutting board, using your sharpest (but not serrated) knife, cut the tuna into ½-inch chunks. (This is easier if the tuna has spent about 15 minutes in the freezer.)

2 Put the tuna in a medium bowl and add the scallions, jalapeño, garlic, ginger, sesame oil, and lime zest. Using a fork, mix to combine, and then with clean hands, form the mixture into 4 patties, each about 1 inch thick. If the mixture is too wet to shape, stir in a teaspoon or two of cornmeal before trying again. Coat the patties with a dusting of cornmeal, cover with plastic wrap, and refrigerate for at least 30 minutes or up to 2 hours.

3 Preheat the grill to high.

4 Grill the patties (in batches, if necessary, depending upon the size of your grill) for about 2 minutes for burgers that are seared on the outside but sushi-style in the middle (or a minute or two longer if you prefer a medium or well-done burger). Top each burger with a spoonful of wasabi mayonnaise before sandwiching in a bun. Serve immediately.

Nutritional values per serving
calories 378; protein 37 g; carbohydrates 26 g; fiber 1 g;
total fat 13 g; saturated fat 2 g; cholesterol 71 mg; sodium 464 mg

Party Pizzas and Pasta Too

Ask all kids what they're in the mood to eat, and pizza is usually on the tip of their tongue. It's no wonder—a doughy crust and melted cheese are the teenage Top Two ingredients. I've had a lot of fun watching my kids and their friends make up new recipes for the Lean Mean Grilling Machine, especially when it comes to pizza. They get downright creative with toppings and surprise me with how good their grilled pizzas can be. Each kid has his or her own style—from crust to toppings to grilling the pizzas. They've taught me some of their tricks, so I feel I've learned from the best.

Pasta shows up on everyone's dinner table—it's a sure bet with the kids and an easy last-minute meal (everyone's got a box of spaghetti in the cupboard). I've got my favorite recipes, but I'll also toss some of my favorite pizza topping combinations into just-cooked pasta. It's a great way to mix it up.

Houston-Not-Hawaii Pizza • Goat Cheese Garden Pizza •
Penne with Grilled Chicken, Portobellos, and Walnuts •
Sweet Sausage with Broccoli Rabe and Bow Ties

Houston-Not-Hawaii Pizza

However Hawaiian this may seem, it was born in my Texas kitchen. Ham steaks take minutes on the grill and pocketless pitas have become our perfect pizza-making material. It was only a matter of time before the two met. This can just as easily become 2 wraps if you use 10-inch flour tortillas instead of pitas and roll them up.

Serves 2 (or 4 as an appetizer)

1 ham steak, about 8 ounces

½ firm but ripe mango

2 teaspoons low-sodium soy sauce

4 ounces shredded Monterey Jack cheese (1 cup)

2 (8-inch) pocketless pitas

1 Preheat the grill to high.

2 Grill the ham steak for 4 minutes, until it has taken on dark grill marks. Transfer to a cutting board and set aside for the moment; keep the grill on high.

3 Grill the mango for 3 minutes, until it is soft and has taken on grill marks. Transfer to the cutting board along with the ham; keep the grill on high and spray with nonstick cooking spray.

4 Cut the ham and mango into bite-sized pieces. Transfer to a bowl, add the soy sauce, and mix to combine. (The ham and mango can be covered and refrigerated overnight. Bring to room temperature before making the pizzas.)

5 Sprinkle the cheese evenly over the pitas, leaving about a ½-inch border around the edge. Divide the ham mixture between the pitas. Grill, one at a time, for about 3 minutes, until the cheese is bubbling and browned in places. Cut in quarters and serve immediately.

Nutritional values per serving

calories 547; protein 43 g; carbohydrates 41 g; fiber 2 g;
total fat 24 g; saturated fat 2 g; cholesterol 101 mg; sodium 2,211 mg

GRILLED PIZZA, 1-2-3

1 The Crust In a break with tradition, there's no kneading a big blob of pizza dough. Pizza on the grill is about fast and store-bought, so we use pocketless pitas or flour tortillas. You can also use a small, pre-baked pizza crust that you've bought at the supermarket. These are a bit thicker, but they also make a fine canvas for your pizza toppings.

2 Toppings The Foreman family classics include: grilled sausage and onions with mozzarella; grilled chicken, tomatoes, sliced olives, and feta; ricotta, grilled red bell pepper, and arugula; Parmesan, Pecorino Romano, and prosciutto with balsamic vinegar; crumbled bacon, lettuce, and tomato over fontina; pepperoni with grilled portobello mushrooms and mozzarella; spicy tomato sauce with canned tuna and red onion slices.

3 Grill Don't forget to spray the top grill with nonstick spray. This prevents the cheese from burning onto the grill and makes cleanup extra easy. The pizza should be grilled just until the cheese melts, so if the other toppings you're using need to be cooked, grill them before layering onto the pizza.

Goat Cheese Garden Pizza

With fresh asparagus and bright cherry tomatoes, this tomato, asparagus, and goat cheese pizza gets veggies into even the most stubborn little—or even big—eaters.

Serves 2 (or 4 as an appetizer)

½ pint cherry tomatoes, cut in half

1 small red onion, sliced

8 medium to thin asparagus spears, woody stems snapped off and discarded

¼ teaspoon dried oregano

¼ teaspoon salt

4 ounces fresh goat cheese, crumbled

2 (8-inch) pocketless pitas

¼ cup walnut pieces

Freshly ground black pepper

1 Preheat the grill to high.

2 Spread the cherry tomatoes onto the grill and cook for about 4 minutes. They will appear almost molten. Spoon into a medium bowl; keep the grill on high.

3 Grill the onion for about 6 minutes, until soft and charred. Transfer to the bowl with the tomatoes; keep the grill on high.

4 Grill the asparagus spears for about 7 minutes, until soft and charred. Transfer to a cutting board; keep the grill on high and spray with nonstick cooking spray. Chop the spears into ½-inch pieces and add to the bowl. Add the oregano and salt to the vegetables and stir to combine.

5 Sprinkle half of the crumbled goat cheese on each of the pitas, leaving about a ½-inch border around the edge. Divide the vegetable mixture between the pitas and top with the walnuts. Sprinkle with pepper.

6 Grill, 1 at a time, for about 2 minutes, until the cheese is bubbling and the vegetables are hot. Cut in quarters and serve immediately.

Nutritional values per serving
calories 211; protein 11 g; carbohydrates 22 g; fiber 2 g;
total fat 11 g; saturated fat 5 g; cholesterol 13 mg; sodium 372 mg

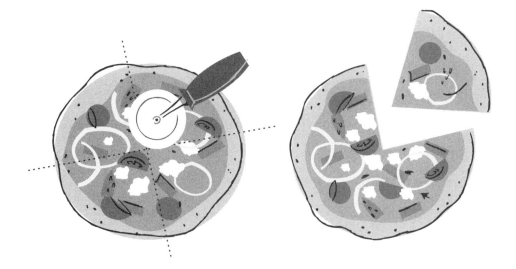

Penne with Grilled Chicken, Portobellos, and Walnuts

My son George loves Italian food. But come to think of it, so do my other sons—George, George, George, and even little George.

This is one great big hearty pasta dish with a little something for everyone: grilled chicken, fresh herbs, delicious portobello mushrooms, and a little bit of crunch from walnuts. Leftovers make a terrific microwaveable workday lunch.

Serves 8

5 portobello mushrooms, stemmed

⅓ cup olive oil

½ teaspoon salt

½ teaspoon freshly ground black pepper

1 pound dried penne

2 pounds boneless, skinless chicken breasts, pounded to ½-inch thickness

¾ cup walnut pieces

½ cup grated Parmesan cheese, preferably freshly grated

¼ cup chopped fresh basil or parsley leaves

2 garlic cloves, minced

1 Preheat the grill to high. Bring a medium pot of salted water to a boil, then reduce to a simmer.

2 Brush the portobellos lightly with a couple of tablespoons of the olive oil and season with ¼ teaspoon of the salt and ¼ teaspoon of the pepper. Grill the mushrooms (in batches, if necessary, depending upon the size of your grill) for about 4 minutes, until the mushrooms are browned and tender. Transfer to a cutting board; keep the grill on high.

3 Bring the water up to a full boil, add the penne, and cook according to the directions on the box.

4 Sprinkle the chicken with the remaining ¼ teaspoon salt and ¼ teaspoon pepper. Grill (in batches, if necessary, depending upon the size of your grill) for about 3 minutes, until it has taken on grill marks and is cooked through. Transfer to the cutting board with the mushrooms.

5 Cut the cooked breasts in half lengthwise and then cut them into ½-inch strips. Slice the portobello caps into pieces approximately the same size.

6 Drain the penne and transfer to a serving bowl. Add the remaining olive oil (about ¼ cup), the mushrooms, chicken, walnuts, Parmesan, basil, and garlic. Toss gently to combine and serve immediately.

Nutritional values per serving
calories 510; protein 41 g; carbohydrates 40 g; fiber 8 g;
total fat 20 g; saturated fat 3 g; cholesterol 70 mg; sodium 301 mg

Sweet Sausage and Broccoli Rabe with Bow Ties

What happens when you take one of the greatest-of-all-time pasta dishes and practically cut out the pasta? Surprisingly, not too much. Our family loves the classic Italian pairing of sweet Italian sausage (most grocery stores have a good version, or you may have a butcher in your neighborhood who makes it fresh) with the distinctive bite of broccoli rabe—leafy stalks and tender florets that are similar to—but not directly related to—the more famous broccoli. The only change we make, besides grilling the components rather than sautéing, is that we cut way back on the pasta. This lower-carb method leaves you with all the great taste and a stick-to-your-ribs feeling, but with fewer carbs. This is one of my favorite pasta tricks.

Serves 4

1 pound sweet fennel sausage (about 5 links)

2 cups dried bow tie pasta

10 ounces broccoli rabe (about ½ bunch)

¼ cup olive oil

3 garlic cloves, minced

½ teaspoon red pepper flakes

½ cup grated Parmesan cheese, preferably freshly grated

1 Preheat the grill to medium. Bring a medium pot of salted water to a boil, then reduce to a simmer.

2 Split the sausages lengthwise and grill (in batches, if necessary, depending upon the size of your grill) for about 6 minutes, until they are firm and cooked throughout. (To check, cut into one of the sausages; there should be no trace of pink left in the center.) Transfer the sausages to a cutting board; keep the grill on but turn to high.

3 Bring the water up to a full boil, add the pasta, and cook according to the directions on the box.

4 In a medium bowl, toss the broccoli rabe with the olive oil and garlic. Grill for about 3 minutes, until the stalks are tender and the leaves have wilted. Transfer to the cutting board with the sausages.

5 Cut the sausages and broccoli rabe into 1-inch pieces. Transfer to a large serving bowl and add the red pepper flakes.

6 Drain the pasta and transfer to the serving bowl. Top with the Parmesan and toss gently to combine. Serve immediately.

Nutritional values per serving
calories 625; protein 31 g; carbohydrates 21 g; fiber 2 g;
total fat 48 g; saturated fat 15 g; cholesterol 109 mg; sodium 1,265 mg

Poultry

There's nothing more convenient than boneless, skinless chicken breasts: they're quick, they're inexpensive, they're healthy, and—marinated or rubbed with spices to give 'em a flavor boost—they're downright delicious. All that makes them America's kitchen champ. From salads to sandwiches, right up to a sit-down dinner, boneless, skinless breasts are the Foreman family's answer to "What's for dinner tonight?"

Pounded thin and grilled on high, chicken breasts take about 3 minutes to cook. When they're done, the chicken breasts will have char-grill marks and feel firm to the touch. You can also check for doneness by slicing into them—the meat should be white with no trace of pink left and the juices should be clear. There isn't a faster, easier, or healthier dinner.

· ·

Do-Anything Lemon Chicken Breasts · Garlic-Herb Chicken Breasts · Chicken Breasts with Nothing-but-Delicious Sauce · Balsamic Rosemary Chicken Breasts · Chicken Curry Salad · Honey-Mustard Chicken Tenders · Montego Bay Jerk Chicken · Coconut Curry Chicken Thighs · Maple Marinated Turkey Breast with Cranberry Compote

Do-Anything Lemon Chicken Breasts

Americans love the ease of boneless, skinless chicken breasts and I'm no exception. I love to punch up the flavor with plenty of fresh lemon juice. These are an instantly tasty main course with Crushed Potatoes (page 186) or Grilled Eggplant with Feta and Lemon (page 176). Sliced, they transform mixed greens into a satisfying main-course salad, and either warm or cold, they're top-notch sandwich material.

Serves 4

> 1 teaspoon grated lemon zest
>
> 1 cup fresh lemon juice (from 5 lemons)
>
> ½ cup olive oil
>
> ½ teaspoon dried oregano
>
> ¼ teaspoon salt
>
> 1 teaspoon freshly ground black pepper
>
> 2 pounds boneless, skinless chicken breasts,
>   pounded to ½-inch thickness

1 Combine the lemon zest, lemon juice, olive oil, oregano, salt, and pepper in a shallow baking dish. Add the chicken breasts, turning to coat. Cover with plastic wrap and refrigerate for at least 30 minutes or overnight.

2 Preheat the grill to high.

3 Grill the breasts (in batches, if necessary, depending upon the size of your grill) for about 3 minutes, until they have taken on grill marks and are cooked through. Serve immediately.

Nutritional values per serving
calories 313; protein 52 g; carbohydrates 1 g; fiber 0 g;
total fat 10 g; saturated fat 2 g; cholesterol 132 mg; sodium 265 mg

Garlic-Herb Chicken Breasts

A marinade really complements the flavor of grilled meats and keeps the meat moist during grilling. Plus, I can prepare the meal the night before and just leave the meat to soak up the marinade. This particular marinade has the deep, intense flavors of dried oregano and thyme as well as the bright taste of fresh rosemary. Add sliced eggplant, tofu, or onion slices to the marinating chicken, and then grill along with the breasts, if you'd like.

Serves 4

½ cup olive oil

3 garlic cloves, minced

1 teaspoon chopped fresh rosemary leaves

1 teaspoon dried oregano

1 teaspoon dried thyme

Grated zest of 1 lemon

¼ teaspoon salt

¼ teaspoon freshly ground black pepper

2 pounds boneless, skinless chicken breasts, pounded to ½-inch thickness

1 In a shallow baking dish, whisk together the olive oil, garlic, herbs, lemon zest, salt, and pepper. Add the chicken breasts, turning to coat. Cover with plastic wrap and refrigerate for at least 2 hours or overnight.

2 Preheat the grill to high.

3 Grill the breasts (in batches, if necessary, depending upon the size of your grill) for about 3 minutes, until they have taken on grill marks and are cooked through. Serve hot or at room temperature. Leftovers make great sandwiches.

Nutritional values per serving

calories 371; protein 52 g; carbohydrates 1 g; fiber 0 g;
total fat 17 g; saturated fat 3 g; cholesterol 132 mg; sodium 148 mg

Chicken Breasts with Nothing-but-Delicious Sauce

While I most often serve this sauce with chicken breasts, it's one of those all-purpose, nothing-but-delicious sauces that dresses up lamb, beef, or most sandwiches. You'll need a blender or food processor to make it properly. The sauce can be made ahead, refrigerated, and then reheated in a saucepan or microwave. Serve this good-looking dish with some Zucchini Antipasto (page 175).

Serves 4

SAUCE

1 medium yellow onion, cut into ½-inch slices

2 large red bell peppers, quartered, cored, and seeded

¼ cup blanched sliced or slivered almonds

¼ cup olive oil

2 garlic cloves

1 teaspoon ground cumin

½ teaspoon cayenne pepper

¼ teaspoon ground ginger

¼ teaspoon salt

1 Preheat the grill to high.

2 Grill the onion slices for 6 minutes, until soft and charred. Transfer to a blender or a food processor; keep the grill on high.

3 Grill the bell peppers for about 6 minutes, until soft and charred. Transfer the peppers to the blender and add the almonds, olive oil, garlic, cumin, cayenne pepper, ginger, and salt. Process, stopping the machine frequently to scrape down the sides with a rubber spatula, until a paste forms. Transfer to a small bowl. (The sauce can be covered with plastic wrap and refrigerated overnight. Bring to room temperature before serving.)

CHICKEN

2 pounds boneless, skinless chicken breasts, pounded to ½-inch thickness

1 tablespoon olive oil

¼ teaspoon salt

½ teaspoon freshly ground black pepper

1 Preheat the grill to high.

2 Coat both sides of the chicken breasts with the olive oil and season with the salt and pepper. Grill the chicken breasts (in batches, if necessary, depending upon the size of your grill) for about 3 minutes, until they have taken on grill marks and are cooked through. Transfer to serving plates, spoon sauce over the breasts, and serve immediately.

Nutritional values per serving
calories 485; protein 55 g; carbohydrates 9 g; fiber 3 g;
total fat 25 g; saturated fat 4 g; cholesterol 132 mg; sodium 389 mg

Balsamic-Rosemary Chicken Breasts

Here are more of America's favorite cuts of chicken finished with a jab of flavor: balsamic vinegar and rosemary. This powerful marinade works well with beef too; try it with a flank or strip steak, or a gorgeous rib eye. Serve the breasts with a simple salad of mixed greens and walnuts or serve as sandwiches on toast with arugula and goat cheese.

Serves 4

½ cup balsamic vinegar

2 tablespoons olive oil

2 rosemary sprigs, coarsely chopped

2 pounds boneless, skinless chicken breasts, pounded to ½-inch thickness

1 Combine the balsamic vinegar, olive oil, and rosemary in a shallow baking dish. Add the chicken breasts and turn to coat. Cover with plastic wrap and refrigerate for at least 30 minutes or overnight.

2 Preheat the grill to high.

3 Grill the chicken breasts (in batches, if necessary, depending upon the size of your grill) for about 3 minutes, until they have taken on grill marks and are cooked through.

Nutritional values per serving
calories 299; protein 52 g; carbohydrates 4 g; fiber 0 g;
total fat 6 g; saturated fat 1 g; cholesterol 132 mg; sodium 152 mg

THE CHAMP'S MONDAY-TO-FRIDAY FAST DINNERS

I love a good strategy, so I like to map out the week's dinners ahead of time. If my day is long—and most are—I'll do a little extra the night before so that when I come home, making dinner won't knock me out, and this way I've got a whole meal on the table in well under 30 minutes.

MONDAY: Chinese New Year Sea Bass (page 166); **Asian Grilled Baby Bok Choy** (page 173); **Cherry Tomato Salad** (page 184); Marinate **Garlic-Herb Chicken Breasts** (page 108) overnight

TUESDAY: Zucchini Antipasto (page 175); **Garlic-Herb Chicken Breasts** (page 108); **Grilled tomato slices** (see page 169); Prepare **Simple Garlic Yogurt Sauce** (page 191)

WEDNESDAY: George's Roasted Asparagus (page 170); **Simple Garlic Yogurt Sauce** (page 191); **Spiced Lamb Burgers** (page 90); Prepare dressing for **Bangkok Beef Salad** (page 128)

THURSDAY: Bangkok Beef Salad (page 128); **Louisiana Banana Split** (page 200); Brine **Apple Cider Pork Chops** (page 134) overnight

FRIDAY: Apple Cider Pork Chops (page 134); **Grilled fennel** (see page 169); **Grilled onion** (see page 169)

Chicken Curry Salad

You can't help but be happy when you come home to this in your fridge. Made ahead of time and chilled, it's great on brown bread and over mixed greens. My wife loves it because it's a very proper ladies' lunch; it's even suitable for tiny tea sandwiches. But this curry salad is no featherweight in the satisfaction department—great texture and terrific flavor make this a universal favorite, for ladies and gentlemen alike.

Serves 4

> *2 pounds boneless, skinless chicken breasts, pounded to ½-inch thickness*
>
> *1¼ teaspoons salt*
>
> *1¼ teaspoons freshly ground black pepper*
>
> *½ cup low-fat plain yogurt*
>
> *½ cup light mayonnaise*
>
> *1½ teaspoons curry powder*
>
> *1 teaspoon ground ginger*
>
> *1 Granny Smith apple*
>
> *½ cup walnut pieces*
>
> *4 iceberg lettuce leaves*
>
> *1 lime, quartered*

1 Preheat the grill to high.

2 Season the chicken breasts with ¼ teaspoon of the salt and ¼ teaspoon of the pepper. Grill the chicken breasts (in batches, if necessary, depending upon the size of your grill) for about 3 minutes, until they have taken on grill marks and are cooked through. Transfer the chicken to a plate and, when cool enough to handle, cut into bite-sized pieces. Transfer to a medium bowl.

3 In a smaller bowl, stir together the yogurt, mayonnaise, curry powder, ginger, remaining teaspoon salt, and remaining teaspoon pepper.

4 Peel and core the apple and cut into ½-inch dice. Add to the chicken along with the walnuts. Stir in the mayonnaise mixture. Cover with plastic wrap and refrigerate for at least 30 minutes or overnight.

5 Spoon the chicken salad over the iceberg lettuce leaves and squeeze some fresh lime juice over each portion before serving.

Nutritional values per serving
calories 441; protein 56 g; carbohydrates 20 g; fiber 2 g;
total fat 15 g; saturated fat 2 g; cholesterol 133 mg; sodium 1,037 mg;

Honey-Mustard Chicken Tenders

Chicken tenders are a relatively new invention that kids go crazy for, but adults seem to enjoy them just as much. The honey-mustard mixture is used as a marinade, but it can also be doubled, leaving half to serve as a dipping sauce. The ground walnuts give these a great crunchy outside without the unwanted fat from deep-frying. (Many doctors recommend that children under three years of age avoid nuts, so leave them out if you're feeding the tiny fellas.) Serve with corn on the cob and it's clean plates all around.

Serves 4

½ cup Dijon mustard

2 tablespoons honey

2 tablespoons olive oil

¾ teaspoon freshly ground black pepper

2 pounds chicken tenders

½ cup walnuts

1 Whisk together the mustard, honey, olive oil, and pepper in a medium bowl. Add the chicken and toss to coat. (The chicken can be grilled immediately or covered with plastic wrap and refrigerated overnight.)

2 Finely grind the walnuts by pulsing them in a food processor or putting them in a heavy-duty plastic bag and pounding them with a rolling pin or heavy skillet.

3 Preheat the grill to high.

4 Toss the chicken tenders in the ground walnuts to coat them lightly.

5 Grill the chicken tenders (in batches, if necessary, depending upon the size of your grill) for about 3 minutes, until they have taken on grill marks and are cooked through. Serve hot, at room temperature, or refrigerate and serve cold.

Nutritional values per serving
calories 444; protein 56 g; carbohydrates 10.5 g; fiber 1 g;
total fat 20 g; saturated fat 3 g; cholesterol 132 mg; sodium 276 mg

Montego Bay Jerk Chicken

People always tell me that one of their favorite things about indoor grilling is that it keeps the kitchen cool even when the temperature outside climbs. This Jamaican jerk recipe is hot all on its own and will satisfy even the most heat-seeking taste buds. The chicken breasts can also be cut into strips and threaded onto skewers and served with Mango Salsa. If you prefer your jerk somewhat less fiery, use one chile instead of two, and discard the seeds. If you've ever rubbed your eyes after chopping chiles, you know from burning experience to wash your hands as soon as you're done handling the chiles.

Serves 4

1 medium yellow onion, chopped

3 scallions, chopped

4 garlic cloves, minced

2 Scotch bonnet or serrano chiles

¼ cup fresh lime juice

3 tablespoons olive oil

2 tablespoons low-sodium soy sauce

1 tablespoon dark brown sugar

1½ teaspoons salt

2 teaspoons freshly ground black pepper

2 teaspoons ground allspice

¾ teaspoon ground nutmeg

½ teaspoon ground cinnamon

2 pounds boneless, skinless chicken breasts pounded to ½-inch thickness

1 cup Mango Salsa (page 182)

1 Combine all of the ingredients except the chicken and the salsa in a shallow baking dish. Add the chicken, turning to coat. Cover with plastic wrap and refrigerate for at least 2 hours or overnight.

2 Preheat the grill to medium.

3 Grill the chicken breasts (in batches, if necessary, depending upon the size of your grill) for about 3 minutes, until they have taken on grill marks and are cooked through. Transfer to serving plates and spoon the mango salsa on top. Serve immediately.

Nutritional values per serving
calories 459; protein 54 g; carbohydrates 30 g; fiber 3 g;
total fat 14 g; saturated fat 2 g; cholesterol 132 mg; sodium 522 mg

Coconut Curry Chicken Thighs

Boxers work hard on legs, and these chicken thighs are no exception. I wanted to get the balance of coconut and curry just right. After I grill the chicken, I'll sometimes pour the marinade into a saucepan, boil for about 5 minutes, and then spoon over a side dish of rice. Fresh cilantro not only lends flavor, but also adds color to the dish—don't skip it!

Serves 4

1 cup canned unsweetened coconut milk

2 tablespoons minced fresh ginger

2 teaspoons curry powder

½ teaspoon salt

¼ teaspoon freshly ground black pepper

2 tablespoons fresh lime juice

2 pounds boneless, skinless chicken thighs

½ cup unsalted roasted cashews, chopped

¼ cup chopped fresh cilantro leaves

1 Whisk together the coconut milk, ginger, curry powder, salt, pepper, and lime juice in a large bowl. Add the chicken, making sure the pieces are completely submerged. Cover with plastic wrap and refrigerate for at least 2 hours or overnight.

2 Preheat the grill to high.

3 Drain the chicken from the marinade, reserving the marinade in a small saucepan if you'd like to make a sauce: bring to a boil on the stovetop and cook until slightly thickened, about 5 minutes.

4 Grill the chicken (in batches, if necessary, depending upon the size of your grill) for about 4 minutes, until it has taken on grill marks and is cooked through. Transfer the chicken to 4 plates, spoon the sauce on top if you've made it, and sprinkle with the cashews and cilantro.

Nutritional values per serving
calories 473; protein 48 g; carbohydrates 7 g; fiber 1 g;
total fat 29 g; saturated fat 14 g; cholesterol 188 mg; sodium 506 mg

Maple Marinated Turkey Breast with Cranberry Compote

I can't tell you how often folks tell me about being separated from their families during the Thanksgiving holiday and how they cook up a version of Thanksgiving dinner for friends on the grill wherever they are. With that in mind, we were driven to give turkey breast cutlets the holiday treatment. Serve this with a salad, store-bought corn bread and a pie, along with a generous helping of friends, and you've got all the fixin's for a holiday meal.

Serves 6

CRANBERRY COMPOTE

½ cup sugar

½ cup water

1 (12-ounce) bag fresh or frozen cranberries

Grated zest and juice of 1 orange

1 tablespoon ketchup

In a medium saucepan, combine the sugar and water. Over medium heat, stir until the sugar has dissolved, about 2 minutes. Add the cranberries, orange zest and juice, and ketchup, and bring to a boil. When the mixture begins to bubble, lower the heat and continue to stir until the berries begin to pop and sauce begins to thicken, about 15 minutes. Transfer to a serving bowl. Let cool to room temperature. (The compote can be covered with plastic wrap and refrigerated overnight. Bring to room temperature before serving.)

TURKEY

¼ *cup olive oil*

¼ *cup pure maple syrup*

8 *fresh thyme sprigs or 1 teaspoon dried thyme*

2 *whole cloves*

¾ *teaspoon salt*

½ *teaspoon freshly ground black pepper*

6 *(6-ounce) boneless, skinless turkey breast cutlets pounded to ½-inch thickness*

½ *cup walnut pieces*

1 In a large shallow baking dish or bowl, combine the olive oil, maple syrup, thyme, cloves, salt, and pepper. Add the turkey cutlets and turn to coat. Cover with plastic wrap and refrigerate for at least 2 hours or overnight.

2 Preheat the grill to high.

3 Grill the turkey cutlets (in batches, if necessary, depending upon the size of your grill) for about 3 minutes, until they have taken on grill marks and are cooked through. Transfer to serving plates, top with the cranberry compote, sprinkle with the walnuts, and serve immediately.

Nutritional values per serving

calories 324; protein 42 g; carbohydrates 30 g; fiber 3 g;
total fat 11 g; saturated fat 2 g; cholesterol 105 mg; sodium 355 mg

Beef, Pork, and Lamb

When I was growing up, my family was so poor that eating meat was a rare occasion. My kids have it different—they're able to enjoy good food every day, and to me, that still means meat.

Beef is my number one favorite. I have it about twice a week and boy, do I enjoy it. A grilled steak is as good as it gets in my book, and I can practically cook one up with my eyes closed. Indoor grilling doesn't only reduce the fat; it reduces the preparation and the guesswork. Pork is the Lean Mean choice. With very little fat, boneless pork chops are the fast and flavorful answer whether counting calories, or counting on a tasty meal. I love the distinctive taste of lamb and especially love what the grill does to lamb skewers or boneless chops.

Spicy Soy Flank Steak • Bangkok Beef Salad • Skirt Steak with Horseradish Cream • Cold Soba with Beef and Cucumber • Apple Cider Pork Chops • Pork Tenderloin with Cucumber-Cashew Salad • Pork Chimichurri • Molasses BBQ Pork Chops • Ham with Orange-Peach Glaze • Creamy Dijon Lamb Chops

Spicy Soy Flank Steak

This is in such demand in our house that I've begun making extra just to have the leftovers, as this is the stuff of supreme sandwiches. For dinner, it's plain old delicious and makes a fabulous, fast weeknight supper. The slightly sweet and spicy sauce can even be made the day before to cut the cooking time. Serve with Cherry Tomato Salad (page 184).

Serves 4

SPICY SOY SAUCE

1 tablespoon olive oil

1 tablespoon minced garlic

1 tablespoon minced fresh ginger

½ cup low-sodium soy sauce

2 tablespoons dark brown sugar

½ teaspoon red pepper flakes

Heat the olive oil in a small saucepan over medium heat. Add the garlic and ginger and, stirring frequently, cook until the garlic begins to brown, about 2 minutes. Add the soy sauce, sugar, and red pepper flakes and bring to a simmer. Cook, stirring occasionally, until a thick glaze forms, about 10 minutes. (The sauce can be cooled, covered, and refrigerated overnight. Reheat before serving.)

FLANK STEAK

1½ pounds flank steak, about 1 inch thick

¼ teaspoon salt

½ teaspoon freshly ground black pepper

1 lime, cut into wedges

1 Preheat the grill to high. Pour half of the spicy soy sauce into a small bowl to use as a glaze. Put the remaining sauce aside.

2 Season the steak on both sides with the salt and pepper. Brush both sides of the steak with some of the sauce from the small bowl. Grill the steak for 2 minutes, then brush the top of the steak with the rest of the sauce in the bowl. Grill for about 3 minutes more for medium-rare. It should have grill marks and feel fairly firm to the touch. Let the steak rest on a cutting board for about 5 minutes before slicing, thinly, across the grain.

3 Divide the slices among 4 plates and drizzle with a spoonful of the reserved sauce. Squeeze some lime juice over each portion and serve immediately.

Nutritional values per serving

calories 350; protein 38 g; carbohydrates 11 g; fiber 0 g;
total fat 16 g; saturated fat 6 g; cholesterol 85 mg; sodium 1,326 mg

Bangkok Beef Salad

This is the way I like to eat. One of the most delicious dishes I know, this Thai-inspired salad of crisp greens, crunchy cashews, and cool cucumbers is built around sliced steak and the tingling saltiness of fish sauce. Besides the fresh healthy ingredients, I also love the applause at the dinner table.

Serves 4

THAI DRESSING

½ cup fresh lime juice (from 4 limes)

2 tablespoons white or cider vinegar

1 tablespoon vegetable oil

1 tablespoon fish sauce

1 garlic clove, minced

2 serrano chiles, seeded and minced

2 tablespoons chopped fresh cilantro leaves

½ teaspoon salt

½ teaspoon sugar

FISH SAUCE In fact made from fish, fish sauce is a fermented vinegar-like condiment with a salty but light, impossible-to-replicate, mouth-watering taste. Available at larger supermarkets, at Asian markets, or online at www.orientalpantry.com.

Whisk together all of the ingredients in a small bowl. (The dressing can be covered and refrigerated overnight.)

BEEF AND SALAD

1 tablespoon vegetable oil

1 tablespoon fish sauce (see box above)

1 tablespoon minced fresh ginger or ½ teaspoon powdered ginger

Grated zest of 2 limes

2 shallots, minced

1 jalapeño pepper, seeded and minced

1 pound London broil or sirloin, about 1 inch thick

2 heads romaine lettuce

1 cucumber, peeled, halved lengthwise, seeded, and thinly sliced

½ pint cherry tomatoes, halved

2 scallions, cut into 2-inch pieces and thinly sliced lengthwise

½ cup unsalted roasted cashews, chopped

1 Preheat the grill to high.

2 Whisk together the oil, fish sauce, ginger, lime zest, shallots, and jalapeño in a small bowl. Coat both sides of the steak with the mixture. Grill the steak for about 5 minutes for medium-rare. It should have grill marks and feel fairly firm to the touch. Let the steak rest on a cutting board for about 5 minutes.

3 Arrange the lettuce leaves on 4 plates. Spread the sliced cucumber and tomatoes over the lettuce. Thinly slice the steak across the grain and arrange over the salad. Whisk the dressing to recombine and drizzle over the meat and greens. Sprinkle the scallions and cashews over the top. Serve immediately.

Nutritional values per serving
calories 382; protein 29 g; carbohydrates 18 g; fiber 4 g;
total fat 24 g; saturated fat 6 g; cholesterol 57 mg; sodium 1,096 mg

Skirt Steak with Horseradish Cream

Skirt steak is not considered an upper cut by most, but I love it. It's flavorful, inexpensive, and perfect for grilling. Experience helps in knowing when a steak is finished cooking. Touch the steak when it's raw, and then feel it after it's cooked on the grill; it should offer resistance and feel somewhat firm, like the heel of your hand.

Serves 4

HORSERADISH CREAM

> *2 tablespoons prepared white horseradish*
>
> *¼ cup light sour cream*

Stir together the horseradish and the sour cream in a small bowl. (The horseradish sauce can be covered with plastic wrap and refrigerated overnight.)

SKIRT STEAK

> *1½ pounds skirt steak, about ¾ inch thick*
>
> *2 tablespoons olive oil*
>
> *¼ teaspoon salt*
>
> *¼ teaspoon freshly ground black pepper*
>
> *2 scallions, white part only, chopped*

1 Preheat the grill to high.

2 Rub the steak on both sides with the olive oil and season with the salt and pepper. Grill the steak for about 4 minutes for medium-rare. It should have grill marks and feel fairly firm to the touch. Let the steak rest on a cutting board for about 5 minutes before slicing, thinly, across the grain. Serve hot or at room temperature, topped with the horseradish cream and scallions.

Nutritional values per serving

calories 395; protein 36g; carbohydrates 3 g; fiber 0 g;
total fat 28 g; saturated fat 9 g; cholesterol 93 mg; sodium 332 mg

Cold Soba with Beef and Cucumber

Made from buckwheat, soba noodles (found in most supermarkets and all Asian markets) have a nutty flavor that's perfect with cool, crisp cucumbers.

Serves 4

SOBA

> *8 ounces soba noodles*
>
> *1 tablespoon sesame oil*

Bring a medium saucepan of water to a boil. Add the soba and cook for about 3 to 5 minutes until it is al dente—soft with just a little firmness left. Drain, rinse with cold water, and transfer to a medium serving bowl. Toss with the sesame oil, cover with plastic wrap, and refrigerate for at least 2 hours or overnight.

STEAK AND DRESSING

> *¾ cup rice vinegar*
>
> *1 tablespoon Asian sesame oil*
>
> *3 garlic cloves, minced*
>
> *1 jalapeño pepper, seeded and minced*
>
> *½ teaspoon salt*
>
> *1 pound flank steak, about 1 inch thick*
>
> *3 tablespoons fresh lime juice (from 2 limes)*

1 Combine the rice vinegar, sesame oil, garlic, jalapeño, and salt in a shallow baking dish. Add the steak, turning to coat. Cover with plastic wrap and refrigerate for at least 2 hours or overnight.

2 Preheat the grill to high.

3 Remove the steak from the marinade, and reserve the marinade in a small saucepan. Grill the steak for about 5 minutes for medium-rare. It should have grill marks and feel fairly firm to the touch. Let the steak rest on a cutting board for about 5 minutes.

4 Bring the marinade to a boil, cook for 1 minute, then remove from the heat. Pour into a small bowl, stir in the lime juice, and refrigerate the dressing to cool while you prepare the salad.

SALAD

1 large seedless cucumber, halved lengthwise and thinly sliced

1 ripe mango, halved and thinly sliced

1 cup chopped fresh basil leaves

1 cup chopped fresh mint leaves

½ cup unsalted roasted cashews, chopped

1 scallion, chopped

SEEDLESS CUCUMBERS

Seedless cucumbers are available in supermarkets, but you can easily remove the seeds from the standard variety: after peeling, cut the cucumber in half lengthwise. Use a teaspoon to scoop out the middle core of seeds.

1 Add the dressing to the soba noodles and toss thoroughly. Add the cucumber, mango, basil, and mint and toss gently to combine.

2 Thinly slice the steak across the grain and arrange over the noodles. Sprinkle the cashews and chopped scallion over the top. Serve immediately.

Nutritional values per serving

calories 577; protein 32 g; carbohydrates 60 g; fiber 6 g;
total fat 25 g; saturated fat 6 g; cholesterol 57 mg; sodium 460 mg

Apple Cider Pork Chops

Brining—an overnight bath in salt water—gives meat moistness and flavor for the most delicious chops on the planet. I add apples and brown sugar to the brine and POW! Take a minute to mix up the brine the night before, soak the meat overnight, and the next day you're 4 minutes away from the best chops you've ever eaten. Crushed Potatoes (page 186) are my top contender for the perfect side dish.

Serves 4

2 cups water

1 cup apple cider

1 small onion,
    roughly chopped

1 apple, roughly chopped

¼ cup salt (remember:
    I always use kosher salt)

¼ cup light brown sugar

3 whole peppercorns

3 fresh thyme sprigs
    or ½ teaspoon dried thyme

4 (6-ounce) boneless center-cut pork chops, pounded to ½-inch thickness

BRINING An old-fashioned method of preserving meats, these days brining is a great way to add flavor, juiciness, and melting tenderness to lean meats such as pork, chicken, and turkey. Let the meat soak in the refrigerator for at least 12 hours or up to 24. The brown sugar in the brine helps the meat get extra brown on the grill (and don't worry; diluted in the liquid, this translates to only a tiny amount of sugar on your chop). Delicious.

1 Combine all of the ingredients except the pork chops in a bowl large enough to hold all of the chops. Stir until the salt and brown sugar dissolve. Add the chops to the brine. Cover with plastic wrap and refrigerate overnight or for up to 24 hours.

2 Preheat the grill to high.

3 Grill the pork chops (in batches, if necessary, depending upon the size of your grill) for about 3 minutes, until the meat has taken on grill marks and is firm to the touch. Serve immediately.

Nutritional values per serving

calories 244; protein 32 g; carbohydrates 1 g; fiber 0 g;
total fat 12 g; saturated fat 5 g; cholesterol 82 mg; sodium 600 mg

Pork Tenderloin with Cucumber-Cashew Salad

When it's hot at home in Houston, this light and tasty meal comes together in a cool flash. The cucumber salad can be made ahead, leaving the grilling of the pork for the last minute. Put the whole, uncooked pork tenderloin into the freezer for about 10 minutes to make slicing a breeze.

Serves 4

2 medium cucumbers, peeled, halved, seeded, and chopped

½ cup salted roasted cashews, chopped

2 scallions, chopped

4 tablespoons olive oil

2 tablespoons sherry vinegar

½ teaspoon freshly ground black pepper

¼ cup chopped fresh basil leaves

2 pounds pork tenderloin

1 In a medium bowl, combine the cucumbers, cashews, scallions, 3 tablespoons of the olive oil, the vinegar, and pepper. Toss well to combine. (The salad can be covered with plastic wrap and refrigerated overnight.) Stir in the basil just before serving.

2 Preheat the grill to high.

3 Cut the pork tenderloin into 8 medallions, each about 1 inch thick, and then pound them to a ½-inch thickness. Rub the remaining tablespoon olive oil over the pork cutlets. Grill (in batches, if necessary, depending upon the size of your grill) for about 3 minutes, until the meat has taken on grill marks and is firm to the touch. Serve each person 2 cutlets with cucumber salad heaped on the top.

Nutritional values per serving

calories 462; protein 51 g; carbohydrates 7 g; fiber 1 g;
total fat 26 g; saturated fat 6 g; cholesterol 147 mg; sodium 182 mg

Pork Chimichurri

One of the healthiest sauces I know, chimichurri can be served with just about any grilled meat. A great Argentine invention (now that's a country that really understands meat), chimichurri has become a part of my regular program, making an appearance in our house at least once a week. Pork tenderloin is a lean, mean cut of meat that I find as versatile as the peppery sauce.

Serves 4

CHIMICHURRI SAUCE

1 large red onion, cut into ½-inch slices

2 red bell peppers, cored, seeded, and cut into 1-inch strips

2 yellow bell peppers, cored, seeded, and cut into 1-inch strips

3 tablespoons olive oil

2 tablespoons white wine vinegar

Juice of 1 lime

1 teaspoon Worcestershire sauce

½ teaspoon red pepper flakes

2 tablespoons chopped fresh parsley leaves

1 Preheat the grill to high.

2 Toss the onion slices and bell pepper strips in 2 tablespoons of the olive oil to coat them lightly. Grill the onion and peppers (in batches, if necessary, depending upon the size of your grill) for about 6 minutes, until soft and charred.

3 Finely chop the peppers and onion in a food processor or by hand using a large sharp knife. Transfer to a medium bowl. Stir in the remaining tablespoon olive oil, the vinegar, lime juice, Worcestershire sauce, and red pepper flakes. (The sauce can be covered with plastic wrap and refrigerated for up to 2 days. Bring to room temperature before serving.) Stir in the parsley just before serving.

PORK

2 pounds pork tenderloin

1 tablespoon olive oil

¼ teaspoon salt

½ teaspoon freshly ground black pepper

1 Preheat the grill to high.

2 Cut the pork tenderloin into 8 medallions, each about 1 inch thick, and then pound them to a ½-inch thickness. Rub the pork cutlets with the olive oil and season with the salt and pepper. Grill (in batches, if necessary, depending upon the size of your grill) for about 3 minutes, until the cutlets have taken on grill marks and are firm to the touch. Serve each person 2 cutlets with the sauce heaped on top.

Nutritional values per serving
calories 446; protein 49 g; carbohydrates 12 g; fiber 3 g;
total fat 22 g; saturated fat 5 g; cholesterol 147 mg; sodium 250 mg

Molasses BBQ Pork Chops

To my mind, homemade barbecue sauce makes all the difference in the world. Store-bought is fine—I've covered a lot of meat with commercial sauce and just grinned when the compliments started—but a sauce you put together yourself is something special. It takes just a few minutes to make the sauce; slather it on your chops, pop 'em on the grill, and you've got dinner in under ten.

Serves 4

MOLASSES BARBECUE SAUCE

  2 tablespoons molasses

  2 tablespoons ketchup

  1 tablespoon cider vinegar

  1 teaspoon light brown sugar

  ¼ teaspoon salt

  Pinch of ground cloves

  Pinch of sweet paprika

Whisk together the molasses, ketchup, vinegar, brown sugar, salt, cloves, and paprika in a small bowl. (The sauce can be covered with plastic wrap and refrigerated for up to 3 days.)

PORK

*4 (6-ounce) boneless center-cut pork chops,
pounded to ½-inch thickness*

1 Preheat the grill to medium.

2 Pour the sauce into a shallow baking dish. Add the chops
and turn to coat. Grill the chops (in batches, if necessary,
depending upon the size of your grill) for about 4 minutes,
until they have taken on grill marks and are firm to the
touch. Serve immediately.

Nutritional values per serving

calories 283; protein 37 g; carbohydrates 10 g; fiber 0 g;
total fat 10 g; saturated fat 3 g; cholesterol 100 mg; sodium 316 mg

Ham with Orange-Peach Glaze

Everyone loves ham with a little sweet something on it—pork and fruit have always been a great team. This strictly southern glaze is best when the peaches are soft and ripe, making this a brunch-worthy midday meal with Creamy Light Coleslaw (page 185) or a light dinner.

Serves 4

- ¼ cup orange marmalade
- ¼ cup Dijon mustard
- 2 tablespoons low-sodium soy sauce
- 1 tablespoon vegetable oil
- ¼ teaspoon freshly ground black pepper
- 2 medium peaches, pitted and cut into 8 wedges
- 2 (8-ounce) ham steaks

1 Preheat the grill to medium.

2 Whisk together the orange marmalade, mustard, soy sauce, oil, and pepper.

3 Grill the peach wedges until they are charred and softened, about 2 minutes. Transfer to a plate; keep the grill on medium.

4 Brush both sides of the ham steaks with the half of the orange glaze and grill (in batches, if necessary, depending upon the size of your grill) for 2 minutes. Brush again on both sides with the remaining glaze and grill for 2 minutes more until the ham steaks have taken on grill marks.

5 Cut each steak in half and divide among 4 plates. Spoon the grilled peaches on top and serve immediately.

Nutritional values per serving
calories 264; protein 23 g; carbohydrates 20 g; fiber 1 g;
total fat 8 g; saturated fat 2 g; cholesterol 51 mg; sodium 2,081 mg

Creamy Dijon Lamb Chops

I love to eat lamb chops but when I've got an army to cook for, chops—which are small, delicate, and a little pricey—aren't right for a hungry crowd. But on those rare occasions when I find myself at dinnertime alone with my wife, these elegant little chops are perfect. Serve with a Cherry Tomato Salad (page 184) and Crushed Potatoes (page 186).

Serves 4

CREAMY DIJON SAUCE

¼ cup Dijon mustard

¼ cup light mayonnaise

1 shallot, minced

1 garlic clove, minced

1 tablespoon Worcestershire sauce

¼ teaspoon salt

½ teaspoon freshly ground black pepper

Whisk together the mustard, mayonnaise, shallot, garlic, Worcestershire sauce, salt, and pepper in a small bowl. (The sauce can be covered and refrigerated overnight. Bring to room temperature before serving.)

LAMB CHOPS

8 (4-ounce) boneless lamb chops, about 1 inch thick

2 tablespoons olive oil

1 teaspoon dried thyme

½ teaspoon salt

½ teaspoon freshly ground black pepper

1 Preheat the grill to high.

2 Rub the chops with the olive oil and then season them on both sides with the thyme, salt, and pepper. Grill the chops (in batches, if necessary, depending upon the size of your grill) for 3 to 4 minutes for medium-rare. The chops will still be rosy in the center.

3 Serve the chops hot off the grill, 2 per person, with the mustard sauce spooned on top.

Nutritional values per serving
calories 385; protein 47 g; carbohydrates 6 g; fiber 0 g;
total fat 16 g; saturated fat 5 g; cholesterol 145 mg; sodium 1,040 mg

Seafood

Even a big Texas beef eater like me loves grilled fish. Besides being loaded with omega-3, a good fat that protects you from everything from cancer to heart disease, fish tastes great too. Light, and satisfying, it's got high-protein punch without anything to slow you down.

Whether you marinate fish fillets, come back from the store with a pound of shrimp, or take on a tuna steak, the grill gets things done without a lot of fuss. And from there, it's as easy as adding a salad and some grilled vegetables for a complete, delicious, and healthy low-carb dinner.

The grill's nonstick surface is especially handy with fish. With a seared outside and a flaky inside, fish is simple on the grill. A lot of folks get intimidated by cooking fish, but once they try it on the grill, they're hooked!

Grilled Popcorn Shrimp • Summer Shrimp Salad • Spanish Shrimp •
Simple Grilled Swordfish • Speedy Salmon with Dijon Glaze •
Tuna with Fresh Tomato-Basil Sauce • Nice Tuna Steaks •
Red Citrus Snapper • Mahi-Mango Salad • Chinese New Year Sea Bass

Grilled Popcorn Shrimp

A famous Cajun snack, popcorn shrimp (so named because—like popcorn—they're eaten by the handful) are usually coated in batter and deep-fried. We love the flavor but can do without the fat, so we've reworked things a bit, keeping the spice but grilling rather than deep-frying. If you've ever tried deep-frying at home, you'll appreciate this recipe not only for its leaner approach, but for its cleaner kitchen factor: there's no greasy mess to clean up afterward. Use this spice rub any time you want to add a little zip to chicken or fish.

Serves 4

SPICE RUB

2 teaspoons garlic powder

2 teaspoons sweet paprika

1 teaspoon onion powder

1 teaspoon dried oregano

1 teaspoon cayenne pepper

1 teaspoon salt

1 teaspoon freshly ground black pepper

1 teaspoon sugar

In a large resealable plastic bag, combine the spices and shake to blend them. (The spice mix can be made ahead and kept nearly indefinitely.)

SHRIMP

*1½ pounds shelled and
deveined small shrimp*

1 lemon, cut into wedges

1 Preheat the grill to high and
spray with nonstick spray.

2 Add the shrimp to the plastic
bag with the spice rub and shake
to coat. Grill the shrimp (in batches, if necessary, depending upon the size of
your grill) for about 3 minutes, until they are opaque and firm to the touch.
Serve the shrimp immediately in a bowl garnished with the lemon wedges
(and with plenty of napkins).

Nutritional values per serving

calories 193; protein 35 g; carbohydrates 5 g; fiber 0 g;
total fat 3 g; saturated fat .5 g; cholesterol 259 mg; sodium 723 mg

> **BUYING SHRIMP** What's sold as "medium" in one store may be "large" in another. But the count—how many shrimp it takes to make a pound—never lies. When buying small shrimp for this recipe, look for those that take about 40 to make a pound. When a recipe calls for medium shrimp, I'm thinking of a 16- to 20-count.

Summer Shrimp Salad

This main course salad is all things to all people. My wife thinks it's the perfect warm-weather dinner and serves it over red-leaf lettuce. My daughter takes it to summer picnics. I like it any time, for any meal, so I'm happy either way.

Serves 4

½ pint cherry tomatoes

3 tablespoons olive oil

½ teaspoon salt

1 pound medium to thin asparagus, woody stems snapped off and discarded

1 pound shelled and deveined medium shrimp

¼ teaspoon freshly ground black pepper

¼ teaspoon dried thyme

Grated zest and juice of ½ lemon

1 Quarter the cherry tomatoes and put them in a medium bowl. Add 1 tablespoon of the olive oil and ¼ teaspoon of the salt. Toss gently and set aside.

2 Preheat the grill to high.

3 In a medium bowl, pour 1 tablespoon of the olive oil over the asparagus spears and rub gently to coat them. Grill the asparagus for about 5 minutes. The thicker ones will still have a bit of crunch to them and the thinner ones will be tender. Transfer to a cutting board; keep the grill on high. When they are cool enough to handle, cut the spears into 1-inch pieces. Add to the cherry tomatoes.

4 Rinse the shrimp and pat dry with paper towels. Put them in a medium bowl, add the remaining tablespoon olive oil, and toss to coat. Grill the shrimp (in batches, if necessary, depending upon the size of your grill) for about 3 minutes, until they are opaque and firm to the touch.

5 Add the shrimp to the tomatoes and asparagus. Add the remaining ¼ teaspoon salt, the pepper, thyme, and lemon juice and zest, and toss to combine. Serve warm or at room temperature, or refrigerate and serve chilled.

Nutritional values per serving

calories 240; protein 25 g; carbohydrates 7 g; fiber 2 g;
total fat 13 g; saturated fat 2 g; cholesterol 172 mg; sodium 408 mg

Spanish Shrimp

Sizzling shrimp is one of our favorite tapas, the little dishes of bite-sized foods served throughout Spain. This is one of those incredibly simple, simply delicious little snacks, similar to Grilled Popcorn Shrimp (page 148), because it's eaten the same way: by the handful. The difference is that these shrimp have a deep garlic flavor.

Serves 4

>   *1½ pounds shelled and deveined medium shrimp*
>
>   *½ cup olive oil*
>
>   *2 garlic cloves, minced*
>
>   *½ teaspoon salt*
>
>   *½ teaspoon red pepper flakes*
>
>   *1 lemon, cut into wedges*

1 Rinse the shrimp and pat dry with paper towels. Combine the shrimp, olive oil, garlic, salt, and red pepper flakes in a medium bowl. Toss gently to combine. Cover with plastic wrap and then refrigerate for at least 30 minutes or up to 2 hours.

2 Preheat the grill to high.

3 Grill the shrimp (in batches, if necessary, depending upon the size of your grill) for about 3 minutes, until they are opaque and firm to the touch. Serve the shrimp immediately in 4 small bowls with the lemon wedges.

Nutritional values per serving
calories 305; protein 35 g; carbohydrates 3 g; fiber 0 g;
total fat 17 g; saturated fat 3 g; cholesterol 259 mg; sodium 487 mg

GEORGE's 3 SIMPLE RULES FOR GOOD FISH

Lots of folks feel that shopping for fish is more difficult than cooking it! It's easy if you keep a few things in mind.

1 Don't purchase fresh fish too far in advance. It's best to cook it on the same day you buy it or the next day at most. It doesn't keep fresh for too long at home.

2 Look for fish with good-looking flesh—no dark spots, bruises, or dull color. Press the fish with your finger: it should feel firm and fit, not spongy. And it should smell clean, with no fishy odor.

3 Frozen fillets should have no grayish signs of freezer burn. Thaw them in the refrigerator overnight and cook on the day the fish has thawed.

Simple Grilled Swordfish

A big steak of a fish, swordfish is another great-for-the-grill way to cook dinner. Simple is the best way to cook most fish—simply grilled with a little olive oil and lemon. Like grilled tuna, swordfish is satisfying and leftovers can be cut into chunks and added to salad for the next day's lunch. (I'll usually cook a little extra just for this purpose.)

Serves 4

4 (6-ounce) swordfish steaks, about ¾ inch thick

¼ cup olive oil

Juice of ½ lemon

½ teaspoon dried oregano

½ teaspoon salt

¼ teaspoon freshly ground black pepper

1 Rinse the fish and pat dry with paper towels.

2 Combine the olive oil, lemon juice, and oregano in a shallow baking dish large enough to fit all the swordfish steaks. Add the swordfish steaks and marinate for about 15 minutes. Turn the steaks and marinate for another 15 minutes.

3 Preheat the grill to high.

4 Sprinkle the swordfish steaks with the salt and pepper. Grill (in batches, if necessary, depending upon the size of your grill) for about 4 minutes. To test for doneness, prod an edge of the swordfish with a fork. The fish should flake easily. Serve immediately.

Nutritional values per serving
calories 327; protein 34 g; carbohydrates 0 g; fiber 0 g;
total fat 21 g; saturated fat 4 g; cholesterol 66 mg; sodium 153 mg

Speedy Salmon with Dijon Glaze

Salmon is a delicious way to get powerful, beneficial nutrition and great flavor on your table. It's one of the most popular fish in America, and almost everybody loves its great texture and taste. This dish is foolproof, even if you've never cooked fish before. Serve it to the family or whip it up for company.

Serves 4

GLAZE

> ¼ cup olive oil
>
> 3 tablespoons low-sodium soy sauce
>
> 2 tablespoons Dijon mustard
>
> 1 shallot, minced

Whisk together the olive oil, soy sauce, mustard, and shallot in a small bowl. Transfer half of the glaze to another small bowl and set aside to spoon over the cooked salmon.

SALMON

4 (6-ounce) skinless salmon fillets, about ¾ inch thick

¼ teaspoon salt

½ teaspoon freshly ground black pepper

1 Preheat the grill to medium.

2 Season the salmon fillets on both sides with the salt and pepper. Put the fillets on the grill (in batches, if necessary, depending upon the size of your grill) and brush them with half of the glaze. Grill for 2 minutes, then brush with the remaining glaze. Grill for about 2 minutes more. To test for doneness, prod an edge of the fillet with a fork. The fish should flake but the center will still be a bit rosy.

3 Serve the salmon either hot from the grill or at room temperature. Drizzle the reserved glaze over the fillets just before serving.

Nutritional values per serving
calories 455; protein 35 g; carbohydrates 2 g; fiber 0 g;
total fat 32 g; saturated fat 6 g; cholesterol 100 mg; sodium 805 mg

Tuna with Fresh Tomato-Basil Sauce

The tomato sauce for this dish requires a little time on the stovetop to make. It adds just the right amount of window dressing for a meal that looks like it was more effort than it was. The sauce is also great over pasta, naturally.

Serves 4

TOMATO-BASIL SAUCE

> *2 tablespoons olive oil*
>
> *1 small yellow onion, diced*
>
> *¼ teaspoon salt*
>
> *½ pint cherry tomatoes, cut in half*
>
> *2 tablespoons water*
>
> *¼ cup fresh basil leaves, chopped*

In a medium saucepan, heat the olive oil over medium heat. Add the onion and salt. Cook, stirring frequently, until the onion is golden brown, 10 to 15 minutes. Add the tomatoes and water and cook for approximately 5 to 7 minutes, until the tomatoes have softened and wrinkled. (The sauce can be cooled, covered, and refrigerated overnight. Reheat before serving.) Stir in the basil just before serving.

TUNA

1 tablespoon olive oil

4 (6-ounce) tuna steaks, about 1 inch thick

1 Preheat the grill to high.

2 Rub the olive oil over the tuna steaks. Grill (in batches, if necessary, depending upon the size of your grill) for about 4 minutes. To test for doneness, prod on edge of the tuna with a fork. The fish should flake, but the center will still be a bit rosy.

3 Spoon the tuna into 4 shallow bowls and top with the warm tomato-basil sauce.

Nutritional values per serving
calories 289; protein 40 g; carbohydrates 3 g; fiber 1 g;
total fat 12 g; saturated fat 2 g; cholesterol 77 mg; sodium 184 mg

Nice Tuna Steaks

Not nice as in nice but nice as in Nice, France. A Niçoise salad is a hearty, healthful meal made up of many of our favorite ingredients: fresh tuna steak, hard-boiled eggs, shiny black olives, and crisp greens.

Serves 4

DRESSING

> ½ cup olive oil
>
> 3 tablespoons red wine vinegar
>
> 1 shallot, minced
>
> 1 garlic clove, minced
>
> ½ teaspoon anchovy paste
>
> ½ teaspoon salt

Whisk together all of the ingredients in a small bowl. (The dressing can be covered and refrigerated overnight.)

TUNA AND SALAD

> ½ pound green beans
>
> 2 heads Boston lettuce, torn into small pieces
>
> 1 pint cherry tomatoes
>
> ½ cup Niçoise or other small black olives
>
> 2 tablespoons chopped fresh basil leaves
>
> 4 (4-ounce) tuna steaks, about 1 inch thick

1 tablespoon olive oil

¼ teaspoon salt

½ teaspoon freshly ground black pepper

2 hard-boiled eggs, peeled and quartered

1 Bring a medium saucepan of salted water to a boil. Add the green beans and cook for 3 to 5 minutes, until tender but still very green. Drain and rinse under cold water until cool. Drain well and transfer to a large bowl. Add the lettuce, tomatoes, olives, and basil to the green beans. Toss gently to combine.

2 Preheat the grill to high.

3 Rub the tuna steaks on both sides with the olive oil and season with the salt and pepper. Grill (in batches, if necessary, depending upon the size of your grill) for about 4 minutes. To test for doneness, prod an edge of the tuna with a fork. The fish should flake, but the center will still be a bit rosy. Transfer to a cutting board.

4 Whisk the salad dressing to recombine, and pour over the salad. Toss gently to coat. Divide the salad among 4 shallow serving bowls or plates, making sure to include a good amount of the tomatoes and olives, which tend to settle at the bottom of the bowl.

5 Cut the tuna into large chunks. Add some of the tuna to each bowl along with half a hard-boiled egg per person and serve immediately.

Nutritional values per serving
calories 501; protein 33 g; carbohydrates 13 g; fiber 4 g;
total fat 37 g; saturated fat 6 g; cholesterol 159 mg; sodium 618 mg

Red Citrus Snapper

Folks usually think we went to a lot of trouble when we serve them this, but the truth is that it couldn't be any easier or faster to prepare. We put the lemon slices that help to flavor the marinade over the fillets before grilling, and the result is downright pretty. Serve this with grilled fennel (see page 169) and rice.

Serves 4

¾ cup orange juice

¼ cup low-sodium soy sauce

2 tablespoons vegetable oil

1 tablespoon Asian sesame oil

3 tablespoons minced fresh ginger or ½ teaspoon ground ginger

4 (8-ounce) skinless red snapper fillets

1 lemon, sliced as thinly as possible

4 scallions, chopped

1 In a shallow baking dish, whisk together the orange juice, soy sauce, vegetable oil, sesame oil, and ginger. Add the red snapper fillets, turning to coat. Spread the lemon slices over the fish. Cover the dish with plastic wrap and refrigerate for at least 30 minutes or up to 2 hours.

2 Preheat the grill to high.

3 Grill the lemon-topped fillets (in batches, if necessary, depending upon the size of your grill) for 2 to 3 minutes. To test for doneness, prod an edge of the red snapper with a fork. The fish should flake easily. Serve immediately, sprinkled with the scallions.

Nutritional values per serving

calories 287; protein 48 g; carbohydrates 8 g; fiber 2 g;
total fat 7 g; saturated fat 1 g; cholesterol 84 mg; sodium 420 mg

Mahi-Mango Salad

he Foremans love mahi-mahi. It's an easy fish to cook, and its satisfying texture is perfect for the way we like to eat. This simple salad can also be used to fill a pita and make a sandwich.

Serves 4

GINGER DRESSING

> *3 tablespoons olive oil*
>
> *Juice of 1 lemon*
>
> *1 garlic clove, minced*
>
> *2 teaspoons minced fresh ginger*

Whisk together all of the ingredients in a small bowl.

SALAD

> *4 (6-ounce) skinless mahi-mahi fillets, about 1 inch thick*
>
> *2 heads Bibb lettuce*
>
> *1 mango, diced*
>
> *1 red onion, halved and thinly sliced*
>
> *½ cup unsalted roasted peanuts, chopped*
>
> *1 tablespoon chopped fresh mint leaves*
>
> *1 tablespoon chopped fresh cilantro leaves*

1 Preheat the grill to high.

2 Grill the fish fillets (in batches, if necessary, depending upon the size of your grill) for about 4 minutes. To test for doneness, prod an edge of the fillet with a fork. The fish should flake easily. Transfer to a cutting board and, when cool enough to handle, cut the fillets into thin strips.

3 Transfer the sliced fish to a large bowl along with the lettuce, mango, onion, peanuts, mint, and cilantro. Drizzle the dressing over the salad. Toss gently to combine before serving the salad in 4 shallow bowls.

Nutritional values per serving
calories 402; protein 38 g; carbohydrates 18 g; fiber 4 g;
total fat 21 g; saturated fat 3 g; cholesterol 125 mg; sodium 159 mg

Chinese New Year Sea Bass

One of our favorite traditional Chinese dishes is sea bass with a soy-ginger-scallion sauce. The traditional preparation calls for steaming the whole fish, but we've tinkered with tradition and come up with this recipe. Serve each fillet with a bowl of sauce on the side to be spooned over. Chinese custom dictates a little rice be served, for luck and prosperity. *Gung hay fat choy!*

Serves 4

> ¾ *cup low-sodium soy sauce*
>
> 3 *tablespoons minced fresh ginger*
>
> 2 *scallions, chopped*
>
> 4 *(6-ounce) skinless sea bass fillets*
>
> ½ *teaspoon freshly ground black pepper*

1 Stir together the soy sauce and ginger in a bowl. Divide among 4 small dipping sauce bowls; top with the scallions.

2 Preheat the grill to high and spray with nonstick cooking spray.

3 Season the sea bass fillets with the pepper. Grill (in batches, if necessary, depending upon the size of your grill) for about 3 minutes. To test for doneness, prod an edge of the sea bass with a fork. The fish should flake easily. Serve immediately with the sauce on the side.

Nutritional values per serving
calories 200; protein 35 g; carbohydrates 5 g; fiber 0 g;
total fat 4 g; saturated fat 1 g; cholesterol 70 mg; sodium 1,201 mg

Vegetables and Greens on the Grill

To me, vegetables are serious business; not only does the government recommend three to five servings daily, I do too! When it comes to healthy choices, vegetables, and plenty of them, should be at the top of everyone's list. From asparagus to zucchini, the nutrition of the Foreman family depends on vegetables, and the grill makes it possible.

Grilling vegetables is the easy fast answer to how to incorporate truly healthy eating into a busy day. A light coating of olive oil makes almost any vegetable grill-ready and delicious. With no water to boil, and no sauté pan to watch, perfectly cooked vegetables are as easy as setting them on the grill for just a few minutes.

George's Roasted Asparagus • Sesame-Scented Asparagus •
Wilted Spinach • Asian Grilled Baby Bok Choy • Grilled Radicchio •
Zucchini Antipasto • Grilled Eggplant With Feta and Lemon •
Stuffed Portobello Caps

THE CHAMP'S GRILLED VEGETABLES

For me, vegetables are center ring at every meal. I serve substantial portions alongside steaks, chicken, or juicy fillets of fish. Besides the fact that they're delicious, we cannot deny the laundry list of health benefits resulting from a diet rich in fresh vegetables. One of my main goals as a parent has been to introduce my kids to a broad variety of vegetables from the earliest possible age, and to keep them coming. This method has been time-tested and seems to have won the battle of ten little Foremans versus their veggies.

Grilling has always been my favorite way to enjoy veggies—and now, with the convenience of indoor grilling, it's as easy as 1-2-3. We rinse and dry the vegetables, coat with a little olive oil, sprinkle them with salt and pepper, and then it's onto the grill. Without heavy pots of boiling water to drain, or spattering sauté pans to contend with, grilled veggies have never been easier. Or more enjoyable.

Our giant dinner table always features several large platters of grilled vegetables—from whatever we have on hand to huge plates bursting with the colors of whatever looked good at the supermarket or farm stand. Or we'll start off a meal with a tray of grilled vegetables with light mayonnaise that we doctor up with minced garlic and lemon zest. Whatever your personal style, there's a way to get grilled vegetables on the table every day.

In addition to the recipes on the following pages, here are some of our favorite ways to grill vegetables:

Bell Peppers In red, green, yellow, and even orange, grilled peppers (see page 58) add both sweetness and color to any plate they're served on. Keep some grilled peppers in the fridge (in a shallow bowl, just covered with olive oil) to add to sandwiches and salads, or to top some plain old buttered toast.

Red Onion Another great way of adding color to a dish, red onions have a wonderful sweetness that's made sweeter by grilling. Slice ½-inch thick, brush with olive oil, and grill until they soften, about 6 minutes.

Fennel After removing the outer leaves of this licorice-flavored bulb, thinly slice the bulb, from the top down to the root end, so that the slices hold together. Brush with olive oil and grill for about 5 minutes on high until the slices have dark char-grill marks. Salads with grilled fennel as well as thinly shaved raw slices are nothing but memorable.

Tomatoes, Both Red and Green Thickly slice the tomatoes and grill for about 3 minutes on high until they're molten and runny. These are beautiful on a mixed platter, perfection alongside grilled meats, and delicious on slices of bread. Don't forget the salt and pepper.

Corn My son cooks corn on the cob on a Lean Mean Grilling Machine. If it's summer and the kernels are particularly sweet and tender, this works well. Shuck the corn, brush with melted butter or olive oil, and grill on high for about 6 minutes, turning halfway through.

Napa Cabbage We love greens that turn tender under the influence of the grill. Separate the large outer leaves, toss lightly in olive oil and vinegar, then grill on medium for about 4 minutes until the leaves look limp.

Broccoli and Cauliflower Broccoli is my constant companion—it's always available, keeps fresh in the fridge for longer than most vegetables, and is the heavyweight champ when it comes to healthy vegetables. I break both broccoli and cauliflower stems into smaller florets, toss in a little olive oil and maybe some soy sauce, and grill them on medium for about 5 minutes, until tender. Eat hot or at room temperature, with a little squeeze of lemon and some freshly ground black pepper.

George's Roasted Asparagus

My favorite way to grill asparagus, it's also the easiest. This recipe gets the vegetable to the table in 7 minutes or less. Freshly grated Parmesan makes everything taste better and this is no exception.

Serves 4

1 pound medium to thin asparagus, woody stems snapped off and discarded

2 tablespoons olive oil

¼ teaspoon salt

½ teaspoon freshly ground black pepper

¼ cup grated Parmesan cheese, preferably freshly grated

1 Preheat the grill to high.

2 Toss the asparagus with the olive oil, salt, and pepper in a medium bowl. Grill the asparagus spears (in batches, if necessary, depending upon the size of your grill) for about 7 minutes, until they have taken on grill marks and are tender. Serve hot or at room temperature, sprinkled with the Parmesan.

Nutritional values per serving
calories 102; protein 4 g; carbohydrates 4 g; fiber 2 g;
total fat 9 g; saturated fat 2 g; cholesterol 4 mg; sodium 212 mg

Sesame-Scented Asparagus

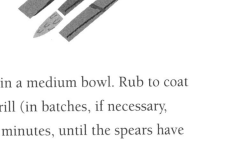

Since asparagus requires next to no preparation, we eat it often. This dish is a simple and tasty way to increase your daily vegetable intake.

Serves 4

> 1 tablespoon Asian sesame oil
>
> 1 pound medium to thin asparagus,
>   woody stems snapped off and discarded
>
> ½ teaspoon salt
>
> 2 teaspoons sesame seeds

1 Preheat the grill to high.

2 Pour the sesame oil over the asparagus spears in a medium bowl. Rub to coat the asparagus. Sprinkle the spears with the salt. Grill (in batches, if necessary, depending upon the size of your grill) for about 7 minutes, until the spears have taken on grill marks and are tender. Transfer to a serving platter and sprinkle with the sesame seeds. Serve hot or at room temperature.

Nutritional values per serving
calories 58; protein 2 g; carbohydrates 4 g; fiber 2 g;
total fat 4 g; saturated fat 1 g; cholesterol 0 mg; sodium 119 mg

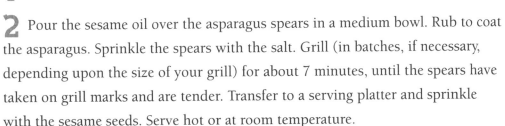

Wilted Spinach

While I don't think that anyone's Italian grandmother made it this way, I find that the Italian classic of sautéed spinach with garlic can be made into a less-mess, less-fat, version cooked on a contact grill. Have the ingredients ready to go, and while a piece of grilled meat is resting, make this your last step before sitting down to dinner.

Serves 4

> *8 ounces fresh baby spinach*
>
> *1 tablespoon olive oil*
>
> *¼ teaspoon garlic powder*
>
> *¼ teaspoon salt*
>
> *1 lemon, halved*

1 Preheat the grill to high.

2 In a medium bowl, toss the spinach with the olive oil, garlic powder, and salt.

3 Spread the spinach in an even layer over the grill. Close the cover and grill for 30 seconds. The leaves should wilt but retain just a bit of crunch. Transfer to a serving bowl and squeeze a bit of lemon juice on top. Serve immediately.

Nutritional values per serving
calories 44; protein 2 g; carbohydrates 2 g; fiber 2 g;
total fat 4 g; saturated fat 1 g; cholesterol 0 mg; sodium 162 mg

Asian Grilled Baby Bok Choy

For a leafy green, bok choy has big personality: strong flavor and texture (this is no delicate lettuce) make it a natural partner for beef. And the light dressing that it's tossed in gives it true Asian flavor. Don't forget to cut the leaves into small bite-sized pieces for the kids.

Serves 4

- *2 tablespoons low-sodium soy sauce*
- *2 tablespoons Asian sesame or vegetable oil*
- *2 garlic cloves, minced*
- *1 tablespoon minced fresh ginger or ½ teaspoon ground ginger*
- *2 heads baby bok choy, about 7 ounces each, leaves separated*

1 Preheat the grill to high.

2 Whisk together the soy sauce, sesame oil, garlic, and ginger in a large bowl. Add the bok choy leaves and toss to coat lightly. Spread the bok choy leaves over the grill (in batches, if necessary, depending upon the size of your grill) and cook for about 3 minutes. The leaves should be tender and bright green. Serve immediately.

Nutritional values per serving

calories 84; protein 2 g; carbohydrates 4 g; fiber 1 g;
total fat 7 g; saturated fat 1 g; cholesterol 0 mg; sodium 336 mg

Grilled Radicchio

Besides lending its unique flavor to grilled fish or meat, radicchio has a brilliant purple color that I like on the plate. Use the wilted leaves as a bed for pork chops, chicken breasts, or Simple Grilled Swordfish (page 154).

Serves 4

> *2 heads radicchio, leaves separated*
>
> *2 tablespoons olive oil*
>
> *2 tablespoons balsamic vinegar*
>
> *¼ teaspoon salt*
>
> *¼ teaspoon freshly ground black pepper*

1 Preheat the grill to high.

2 In a large bowl, toss the radicchio leaves with the oil, vinegar, salt, and pepper. Spread the leaves in an even layer over the grill. Grill for about 2 minutes until the leaves are wilted. Serve immediately.

Nutritional values per serving

calories 79; protein 1 g; carbohydrates 4 g; fiber 1 g;
total fat 7 g; saturated fat 1 g; cholesterol 0 mg; sodium 129 mg

Zucchini Antipasto

I love the Italian custom of serving grilled vegetables before the main meal. This grilled zucchini dish works with any of the grilled main course meats or fish in this book, but served alongside some sliced mozzarella, tomatoes, and olives, this is a pretty-as-a-picture appetizer or party food, a great way to begin an evening with friends.

Serves 4

> ¼ cup olive oil
>
> 3 garlic cloves, minced
>
> 1 tablespoon fresh thyme leaves or ½ teaspoon dried thyme
>
> ¼ teaspoon salt
>
> ¼ teaspoon freshly ground black pepper
>
> 4 medium zucchini, cut lengthwise into ¼-inch-thick slices
>
> 1 tablespoon balsamic vinegar

1 Preheat the grill to high.

2 Whisk together the olive oil, garlic, thyme, salt, and pepper in a large bowl. Add the zucchini and toss to coat. Grill (in batches, if necessary, depending upon the size of your grill) for about 6 minutes, until the zucchini slices have taken on grill marks and are very tender. Serve either hot off the grill or at room temperature, sprinkled with the vinegar.

Nutritional values per serving
calories 156; protein 2 g; carbohydrates 8 g; fiber 2 g;
total fat 14 g; saturated fat 2 g; cholesterol 0 mg; sodium 125 mg;

Grilled Eggplant with Feta and Lemon

Eggplant is one of those do-it-all grilled vegetables—slices of grilled eggplant can go onto sandwiches, be served as is next to grilled meats, or be pulverized with garlic and mint to make a quick dip. Eggplant is nutritious, filling, and available year-round. That means we serve a lot of it. For a first course or a side dish, this Greek-style recipe always pleases.

Serves 4

1 large eggplant, cut into ½-inch slices

1 tablespoon salt

3 tablespoons olive oil

4 ounces feta cheese, crumbled

½ teaspoon sweet paprika

Freshly ground black pepper

1 lemon, cut in half

1 Spread the eggplant slices on a rimmed baking sheet and sprinkle with half of the salt. Flip the slices and sprinkle with the remaining salt. Let sit for 15 minutes to take away some of the bitterness of the eggplant. Transfer the slices to sheets of paper towels and pat dry.

2 Preheat the grill to high.

3 Brush both sides of the eggplant slices with the olive oil. Grill (in batches if necessary, depending upon the size of your grill) for about 6 minutes, until the slices have taken on grill marks and are golden brown. Transfer the eggplant to a serving platter and top with the feta, paprika, some pepper, and a squirt of lemon juice. Serve hot or at room temperature.

Nutritional values per serving
calories 204; protein 6 g; carbohydrates 11 g; fiber 4 g;
total fat 17 g; saturated fat 6 g; cholesterol 25 mg; sodium 1,731 mg

Stuffed Portobello Caps

Serve this "sandwich" of goat-cheese-stuffed portobello caps as a great vegetarian entrée, or slice the caps into wedges for finger food.

Serves 4

   4 medium portobello mushroom caps

   6 ounces fresh goat cheese

   ½ cup store-bought pesto

   ¼ cup walnut pieces

   ¼ teaspoon salt

   2 tablespoons olive oil

1 Slice the mushroom caps in half horizontally. Open the halves and spread them out on a clean work surface.

2 Using a fork, combine the goat cheese, pesto, walnuts, and salt in a medium bowl. Spread the goat cheese mixture evenly over the 4 bottom halves of the mushrooms. Cover with the tops, and brush the tops lightly with the olive oil.

3 Preheat the grill to high and spray with nonstick cooking spray.

4 Grill the stuffed mushrooms for 4 to 5 minutes, until the mushrooms are golden brown and the goat cheese is warm. Serve immediately.

Nutritional values per serving
calories 407; protein 15 g; carbohydrates 10 g; fiber 2 g;
total fat 36 g; saturated fat 10 g; cholesterol 25 mg; sodium 502 mg

On the Side

These are a few of our family's favorite ways to round out a meal. Fresh salads, fruit salsas, and even a potato dish let us fill up our dinner plates with a variety of grilled and fresh homemade food. Plus, sometimes we've just gotta give the grill a rest!

Simple Guacamole • Watermelon Salsa • Mango Salsa •
Cherry Tomato Salad • Creamy Light Coleslaw • Crushed Potatoes

Simple Guacamole

I'm a believer in the less-is-more school of guacamole making; I don't come on heavy with tomatoes, salsas, or sour cream. Guacamole's success lies almost entirely in using the right avocados: perfectly ripe ones with the roughly textured, dark green skin. Squeeze them gently before buying and select those that are soft but not mushy. The still-firm ones will soften over the course of a few days at room temperature.

Makes 2 cups

> *4 ripe avocados*
>
> *1 medium red onion, diced*
>
> *¼ cup chopped fresh cilantro leaves*
>
> *Juice of 1 lime*
>
> *1 teaspoon salt*
>
> *Dash of hot sauce*

Cut the avocados in half and remove the pit. Scoop the flesh into a medium bowl and add the remaining ingredients. Use a fork to mash the avocado and combine with the other ingredients. This is best served within a couple of hours, before the avocado starts to discolor.

Nutritional values per serving
calories 160; protein 2 g; carbohydrates 8 g; fiber 5 g;
total fat 15 g; saturated fat 2 g; cholesterol 0 mg; sodium 247 mg

Watermelon Salsa

This is so delicious that we serve it all summer long with almost everything. There are few things better with grilled meat and, as an added benefit, watermelon always makes people smile. This can be made 2 hours before eating, but it will get watery if it sits longer than that.

Makes about 3½ cups

- *2 pounds seedless watermelon, rind removed, flesh cut into 1-inch cubes (about 2 cups)*
- *½ medium red onion, finely chopped*
- *⅓ cup chopped fresh cilantro leaves*
- *1 jalapeño pepper, minced*
- *2 tablespoons fresh lime juice*
- *1 teaspoon salt*

Place all of the ingredients into a medium bowl and toss gently to combine. This is best served within a couple of hours.

Nutritional values per ½-cup serving
calories 47; protein 1 g; carbohydrates 11 g; fiber 1 g;
total fat .5 g; saturated fat 0 g; cholesterol 0 mg; sodium 273 mg

Mango Salsa

This is cooked stovetop for a sweet-hot flavor that blends a small amount of brown sugar and jalapeño. Naturally it's served with all manner of grilled meats (especially Montego Bay Jerk Chicken, page 118), but it's an extra-special dip for tortilla chips. If you don't want to turn on the stove, omit the brown sugar and orange juice and mix the rest of the ingredients for a fresh, no-cook salsa.

Makes about 2 cups

2 tablespoons olive oil

2 medium yellow onions, diced

1 garlic clove, minced

1 teaspoon minced fresh ginger

2 ripe mangoes, cut into small dice

1 jalapeño pepper, seeded and minced

¼ cup orange juice

1 tablespoon light brown sugar

½ teaspoon salt

½ teaspoon freshly ground black pepper

2 teaspoons chopped fresh mint leaves

1 In a medium sauté pan, heat the olive oil over medium heat. Add the onions and cook, stirring occasionally, until translucent, 8 to 10 minutes. Stir in the garlic and ginger and cook for 1 minute more. Add the mangoes and jalapeño, lower the heat, and simmer gently for about 10 minutes, until the mangoes have softened.

2 Add the orange juice, brown sugar, salt, and pepper. Continue to simmer, stirring from time to time, until there is no more liquid left in the pan, about 5 minutes. Transfer to a bowl and stir in the mint. Serve hot, at room temperature, or chilled. (The salsa can be cooled, covered, and refrigerated overnight.)

Nutritional values per serving

calories 85; protein 1 g; carbohydrates 14 g; fiber 1.5 g;
total fat 4 g; saturated fat .5 g; cholesterol 0 mg; sodium 120 mg

Cherry Tomato Salad

Cherry tomatoes are always in the stores and have a consistent, great flavor throughout the year. I almost always have a pint in the refrigerator, making this salad a regular in our house. They also add great color to any main dish. Let the tomatoes sit for up to an hour before serving to allow the salt to draw some liquid from the tomatoes and make the dressing taste even better.

Serves 4

1 pint cherry tomatoes, quartered

1 teaspoon salt

½ teaspoon freshly ground black pepper

¼ cup olive oil

3 tablespoons sherry vinegar

5 fresh basil leaves, cut into thin slivers

¼ cup grated Parmesan cheese, preferably freshly grated

1 In a medium bowl, gently toss the tomatoes with the salt and pepper. If you have the time, set the tomatoes aside for an hour or so before dressing them; this will help draw out their juices and make the salad even more flavorful.

2 Whisk together the oil and vinegar in a small bowl. Add to the tomatoes along with the fresh basil and toss to combine. Serve at room temperature or chilled. Top each serving with a sprinkling of Parmesan.

Nutritional values per serving
calories 164; protein 3 g; carbohydrates 4 g; fiber 1 g;
total fat 16 g; saturated fat 3 g; cholesterol 4 mg; sodium 571 mg

Creamy Light Coleslaw

Make it ahead so the flavors have a chance to get to know one another. Serve it cold so it refreshes. In our house, homemade coleslaw, a great American achievement, is a requirement at family picnics, buffets, and sandwich lunches. I love to mix purple and green cabbages for a great look at the table.

Serves 6

1 cup light mayonnaise

¼ cup sherry vinegar

1 teaspoon caraway seeds

¼ teaspoon salt

1 teaspoon freshly ground black pepper

1 small head cabbage

3 large carrots

1 Whisk together the mayonnaise, vinegar, caraway seeds, salt, and pepper in a large serving bowl.

2 Quarter and core the cabbage. Shred in a food processor or thinly slice by hand. Transfer to the serving bowl. Shred the carrots in a food processor or grate on the large holes of a box grater. Add the carrots to the bowl. Toss to coat and refrigerate until ready to serve or overnight.

Nutritional values per serving
calories 184; protein 2 g; carbohydrates 13 g; fiber 4 g;
total fat 14 g; saturated fat 3 g; cholesterol 13 mg; sodium 420 mg

Crushed Potatoes

This lies somewhere between mashed potatoes and potato salad—it's delicious warm or at room temperature. This is perfect with grilled meats, but don't forget a green veggie! If you'd like to turn this into a potato salad, dice the potatoes instead of crushing them and add 3 tablespoons balsamic vinegar and 2 chopped shallots. It couldn't be easier.

Serves 4

1¼ pounds Yukon Gold potatoes (about 3 medium to large)

¾ teaspoon salt

¼ cup olive oil

¼ teaspoon freshly ground black pepper

1 Put the potatoes in a large pot and add water to cover by at least an inch. Add ½ teaspoon of the salt and bring to a boil. Cook for about 20 minutes, until the potatoes are easily pierced with a fork. Drain well and set aside to cool slightly.

2 When the potatoes are cool enough to handle, peel them and discard the skins. Put the potatoes in a medium bowl. Using a fork, crush the potatoes. Add the olive oil, the remaining ¼ teaspoon salt, and the pepper. Continue to press the potatoes with the fork until they are almost mashed and have absorbed the olive oil. Serve warm or at room temperature.

Nutritional values per serving
calories 222; protein 3 g; carbohydrates 22 g; fiber 2 g;
total fat 14 g; saturated fat 2 g; cholesterol 0 mg; sodium 244 mg;

Sauces, Spice Rubs, and Marinades

Marinades, spice rubs, and sauces are the simple way to take one type of meat and make it taste a hundred different ways. The simple marinades in this chapter and those throughout this book offer plenty of options. Meat can marinate overnight, but seafood should marinate up to 2 hours only (otherwise the texture starts to suffer). Combine the ingredients in a nonreactive (glass or ceramic) shallow baking dish or a large resealable plastic bag.

Sauces are another way to layer on flavor as meat is cooking or after it's already done, from barbecue sauce to ginger dipping sauce. A little sauce mixed up in advance adds a fresh-made touch to food.

Championship Chipotle BBQ Sauce • Texas 2-Step Sauce •
Ginger Dipping Sauce • Simple Garlic Yogurt Sauce •
Spicy Spanish Rub • Brown Sugar Spice Rub • Mediterranean Marinade •
Island Marinade • Asian Marinade • Curry-in-a-Hurry Marinade •
Fiery Western Beef Marinade

Championship Chipotle BBQ Sauce

For those who want a barbecue sauce with more kick to it, this is the ticket. Chipotle chiles add fire without the flame.

Makes about 1¼ cups

1 cup ketchup

2 tablespoons butter, at room temperature

1 garlic clove, minced

1 tablespoon Worcestershire sauce

1 teaspoon chipotle puree (see page 83)

1 teaspoon salt

½ teaspoon freshly ground black pepper

Whisk together all of the ingredients in a small bowl. (The sauce can be covered with plastic wrap and refrigerated for 1 week. Bring to room temperature and whisk again to recombine before serving.)

Nutritional values per 2-tablespoon serving
calories 48; protein .5 g; carbohydrates 6.5 g; fiber 0 g;
total fat 2.5 g; saturated fat 1.5 g; cholesterol 6 mg; sodium 564 mg

Texas 2-Step Sauce

The 2 steps are mix and refrigerate. This barbecue sauce can be kept in your refrigerator for up to a week so it's on hand and ready to come out swingin' to jazz up beef or pork. It's a unanimous decision: Texas 2-Step turns an ordinary chop into a champ.

Makes about 1½ cups

1 cup ketchup

¼ cup light brown sugar

2 garlic cloves, minced

3 tablespoons Worcestershire sauce

2 tablespoons cider vinegar

2 teaspoons salt

1 teaspoon freshly ground black pepper

1 teaspoon dried oregano

In a medium bowl, whisk together all of the ingredients until the brown sugar has dissolved and the mixture is smooth. (The sauce can be covered with plastic wrap and refrigerated for a week.)

Nutritional values per 2-tablespoon serving
calories 43; protein 1 g; carbohydrates 10 g; fiber 0 g;
total fat 1 g; saturated fat 0 g; cholesterol 0 mg; sodium 639 mg

Ginger Dipping Sauce

Delicious with Sirloin Beef Brochettes with Honey-Soy Marinade (page 22) or even spooned over sliced steak, this is the sauce any time you want to add a slightly sweet, tangy Asian jab of flavor to beef.

Makes about 1 cup

¼ cup minced fresh ginger

¼ cup low-sodium soy sauce

¼ cup rice vinegar

3 tablespoons honey

Whisk together all of the ingredients in a small bowl. (The sauce can be covered with plastic wrap and refrigerated for up to 3 days. Bring to room temperature and whisk again to recombine before serving.)

Nutritional values per 2-tablespoon serving

calories 33; protein 1 g; carbohydrates 8 g; fiber 0 g;
total fat 0 g; saturated fat 0 g; cholesterol 0 mg; sodium 272 mg

Simple Garlic Yogurt Sauce

Serve this as a condiment with grilled lamb or kebabs. The chopped mint gives it a cool freshness that complements the grilled meat. It's also a great dip for raw fresh vegetables.

Makes about 1 cup

1 cup Greek yogurt

3 garlic cloves, minced

½ teaspoon salt

¼ cup chopped fresh mint leaves

GREEK YOGURT is thicker and richer with a more pronounced flavor than regular yogurt and it's sold in most large supermarkets. If you can't find Greek yogurt, put regular yogurt in a paper-towel-lined strainer set over a bowl and let it drain in the refrigerator for about 4 hours until thickened. You'll need to start with about 1¼ cups regular yogurt to end up with 1 cup for this recipe.

Stir together the yogurt, garlic, and salt in a small bowl. (The sauce can be covered with plastic wrap and refrigerated for up to 3 days.) Stir in the mint just before serving. Serve chilled or at room temperature.

Nutritional values per 2-tablespoon serving
calories 18; protein 2 g; carbohydrates 1.5 g; fiber 0 g;
total fat .5 g; saturated fat .4 g; cholesterol 1 mg; sodium 137 mg

Spicy Spanish Rub

There are plenty of commercially prepared spice rubs on the market, but making your own is easy, allows you to adjust the flavor to suit your taste (if you love paprika, add a little more), and is the best way to ensure that the spices are still fresh. This particular one is hot stuff, so a little goes a long way. Coat chicken, pork, shrimp, fish, or vegetables with this spice rub and pop 'em right on the grill.

Makes enough to coat 2 pounds of meat, seafood, or vegetables

1½ teaspoons curry powder

¼ teaspoon ground cumin

¼ teaspoon ground paprika

¼ teaspoon ground coriander

Combine all of the spices in a glass jar or resealable plastic bag. Shake to mix well. Stored in a cool, dark place, this keeps nearly indefinitely.

Brown Sugar Spice Rub

This rub adds a smoky-sweet-and-spicy flavor to beef and pork and uses just a touch of brown sugar.

Makes enough to coat 2 pounds of meat

2 tablespoons ground cumin

1 tablespoon dried oregano

1 tablespoon freshly ground black pepper

1 tablespoon light brown sugar

1½ teaspoons ground cinnamon

1½ teaspoons sweet paprika

1 teaspoon salt

Combine all of the spices in a glass jar or resealable plastic bag. Shake to mix well. Stored in a cool, dark place, this keeps nearly indefinitely.

Mediterranean Marinade

This gets the prize for Most Popular Marinade. The ingredients are in almost everybody's kitchen already, and the marinade has great garlicky flavor. Any piece of chicken, beef, or fish that's done some time in it becomes juicier and more delicious.

Makes enough to coat 2 pounds of meat or seafood

½ cup olive oil

¼ cup chopped fresh herbs (such as parsley, rosemary, thyme, and oregano leaves)

3 garlic cloves, crushed

Grated zest of 1 lemon

½ teaspoon salt

½ teaspoon freshly ground black pepper

Whisk together all of the ingredients. (The marinade can be covered and refrigerated for a couple of days before using.)

Island Marinade

When we wish we were in the Caribbean, we add a little chicken or fish to this marinade. It almost works, but the water isn't quite as blue in Houston!

Makes enough to coat 2 pounds of meat or seafood

1 cup canned unsweetened coconut milk

½ cup chopped fresh cilantro leaves

3 garlic cloves, crushed

2 tablespoons minced fresh ginger

Juice of 1 lime

Whisk together all of the ingredients. (The marinade can be covered and refrigerated for a couple of days before using.)

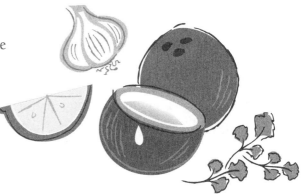

Asian Marinade

With Asian flavors becoming more and more popular in restaurants, I love to serve beef or chicken that's been soaked in this homemade sweet and sour marinade. It's one way I keep 'em coming home for dinner!

Makes enough to coat 2 pounds of meat or seafood

1/4 cup vegetable oil

5 garlic cloves, crushed

3 tablespoons fish sauce (see box on page 128)

2 tablespoons Asian sesame oil

2 tablespoons low-sodium soy sauce

2 teaspoons sugar

1 teaspoon grated lime zest

Whisk together all of the ingredients. (The marinade can be covered and refrigerated for a couple of days before using.)

Curry-in-a-Hurry Marinade

I find myself craving curry—I just love the taste. This is one of the ways I mix it up in the home kitchen with Indian spices. Chicken or lamb works great with this yogurt marinade.

Makes enough to coat 2 pounds of meat

    2 cups low-fat plain yogurt

    1 medium yellow onion, quartered

    1 garlic clove, crushed

    1 jalapeño pepper, sliced

    1 tablespoon curry powder

    1 teaspoon ground fennel seeds

    1 teaspoon salt

    ½ teaspoon freshly ground black pepper

Whisk together all of the ingredients. (The marinade can be covered and refrigerated for a couple of days before using.)

Fiery Western Beef Marinade

Here's another marinade with ingredients that are probably in your kitchen right now. I give steaks a good overnight rest in this big-flavor mix.

Makes enough to coat 2 pounds of meat

½ cup olive oil

¼ cup Dijon mustard

3 tablespoons Worcestershire sauce

2 garlic cloves, minced

3 dashes hot sauce

Whisk together all of the ingredients. (The marinade can be covered and refrigerated for a couple of days before using.)

A Little Dessert

While I'm not much into desserts (I think a piece of fruit after a meal is the way to go), I do indulge every once in a while. And, like all kids, mine love a treat for cleaning their plates. So the end of dinner in the Foreman house usually starts with grilled fruit.

Grilling fruit brings out the sweetness, and when you layer the warm fruit with cold yogurt or ice cream, the à la mode combination is winning. Tropical fruits like pineapple, mango, or star fruit are especially good on the grill. We brush them with honey, sprinkle with a little brown sugar, or just plain slice and grill them. We love them on their own, or built into a more special dessert. Summer nectarines and peaches turn soft and even sweeter after a few minutes on the grill. (My daughter grills a slice of pound cake to toast it, piles grilled peaches on top, and calls it fruitcake!) And grilled figs can get the dessert treatment or turn up on a dinner plate with pork chops. As always, it's all about versatility—and ease. So clear the dishes, and fire up the grill again . . . it's time for dessert.

Louisiana Banana Split · Honey-Glazed Pineapple · Grilled Nectarines with Blackberries and Mascarpone · Chocolate Chip Hot Tarts

Louisiana Banana Split

This is the Foreman version of the New Orleans classic, Bananas Foster.
Serves 4

2 tablespoons unsalted butter

1 tablespoon dark brown sugar

½ teaspoon vanilla extract

¼ teaspoon ground cinnamon

2 bananas, peeled and halved lengthwise

4 scoops low-fat vanilla frozen yogurt

¼ cup walnut pieces

1 Combine the butter, brown sugar, vanilla, and cinnamon in a small saucepan. Warm over low heat, stirring until the butter melts and the brown sugar dissolves.

2 Preheat the grill to medium.

3 Brush the banana halves with the melted-butter mixture. Grill (without lowering the top grill) for 1 minute, then brush the bananas again with the melted butter. Flip the bananas and grill for 1 minute more until hot.

4 Transfer the bananas to shallow bowls and top each with a scoop of frozen yogurt. Sprinkle with the walnuts and drizzle the remaining melted-butter mixture on top. Serve immediately.

Nutritional values per serving
calories 369; protein 11 g; carbohydrates 50 g; fiber 2 g;
total fat 15 g; saturated fat 7 g; cholesterol 81 mg; sodium 57 mg

Honey-Glazed Pineapple

Pineapple is delicious grilled, and while you can add a scoop of vanilla ice cream if you like, we eat it just on its own. Remember *fresh*—canned pineapple just won't do.

Serves 4

1 small ripe pineapple

¼ cup honey

¼ cup fresh lime juice

1 tablespoon light brown sugar

2 tablespoons chopped fresh mint leaves

1 To peel the pineapple, use a large serrated knife to cut off the bottom and top. Stand the pineapple on one end on a cutting board and begin cutting the skin away from the top toward the bottom. Rotate the pineapple on the board until all of the skin has been removed.

2 Cut the pineapple into slices about ¾ inch thick. Use a paring knife to remove the core and then transfer the slices to a shallow baking dish.

3 Combine the honey and lime juice in a small bowl. Spoon the honey mixture over the pineapple, using the back of the spoon to spread the honey over all of the slices. Turn the slices over to coat both sides. Let the slices marinate for at least 1 hour or up to 8.

4 Preheat the grill to medium.

5 Sprinkle the brown sugar over the slices. Grill for about 3 minutes, until golden brown. Serve hot or at room temperature, sprinkled with the mint.

Nutritional values per serving

calories 135; protein .5 g; carbohydrates 35 g; fiber 2 g;
total fat .5 g; saturated fat 0 g; cholesterol 0 mg; sodium 2 mg

Grilled Nectarines with Blackberries and Mascarpone

Mascarpone is a slightly sweet but tangy soft cheese. Sold in most supermarkets (near the sour cream and cottage cheese), mascarpone makes a great topping for most fruits, particularly berries.

Serves 4

2 tablespoons honey

2 large ripe nectarines, quartered

½ teaspoon ground cinnamon

1 pint blackberries, blueberries, raspberries, or strawberries (if using strawberries, thinly slice them)

¼ cup mascarpone

1 Preheat the grill to medium.

2 Spoon the honey into a small shallow baking dish. Dip the nectarine sections into the honey and then sprinkle the flesh side with the cinnamon. Grill the nectarines, flesh side down, for about 3 minutes, until the flesh is crisp, hot, and browned. Serve the nectarines in shallow bowls, topped with the berries and a spoonful of mascarpone.

Nutritional values per serving

calories 162; protein 1 g; carbohydrates 25 g; fiber 5 g;
total fat 7 g; saturated fat 5 g; cholesterol 18 mg; sodium 5 mg

Chocolate Chip Hot Tarts

These warm, gooey chocolate sandwiches, which started as a rainy-day experiment in our house, have become the favorite after-school treat of my youngest son, George VI, and his friends.

Serves 4

4 slices white bread, crusts removed

2 teaspoons butter, at room temperature

8 teaspoons semisweet chocolate chips

4 teaspoons walnut pieces

1 Preheat the grill to high.

2 With a rolling pin or the palms of your hands, roll or press the bread slices until they are flat and compressed. Butter the bread and turn over the slices. Sprinkle 2 teaspoons of chocolate chips and 1 teaspoon of walnuts over half of each slice of bread. Fold the empty halves over the filling and gently press to close.

3 Use a spatula to transfer the sandwiches to the grill. Grill for about 3 minutes, until the chocolate melts and the sandwiches are golden brown. Serve immediately.

Nutritional values per serving
calories 133; protein 3 g; carbohydrates 17 g; fiber 1 g;
total fat 6 g; saturated fat 3 g; cholesterol 5 mg; sodium 136 mg

First Thing in the A.M.

I've never had breakfast in bed. During my tough training as a world champion boxer, I got used to getting up early. Real early. It was not only good training in the ring, it was good training for being a father—those babies get up at daybreak! Or at least some of them do. Making breakfast always falls to the early riser, and in my family that's me.

So that means the grill gets going early as well. During the week we'll use it for bacon or sausage, or my high-protein breakfast patties, served alongside eggs and whole grain cereals. On Sunday, we'll go for a more special breakfast before church and use the grill for French toast or grilled breakfast sandwiches. With all the breakfast I have to cook, it's a good thing I'm not a late sleeper. I guess I'm just not a breakfast-in-bed kind of guy.

Pork and Apple Breakfast Patties • Chicken and Sun-Dried Tomato Sausage Patties • Good Morning Pork and Turkey Sausage Patties • Smoked Salmon Croque Monsieur • Tofu "Huevos Rancheros" • Pumpkin French Toast • Mango Breakfast Parfait

Pork and Apple Breakfast Patties

While this could be mistaken for a midday hamburger, we have it for breakfast with a fried egg on top. It's a flavorful, protein-packed way to start the day.

Makes 8 patties; serves 4

  2 large egg whites

  1 apple, peeled and diced

  ¼ cup chopped dried apricots or prunes

  2 scallions, chopped

  2 garlic cloves, minced

  1 teaspoon salt

  ½ teaspoon freshly ground black pepper

  ¼ teaspoon ground nutmeg

  1 pound lean ground pork

1 In a large bowl, beat the egg whites until frothy. Stir in the apple, chopped fruit, scallions, garlic, salt, pepper, and nutmeg.

2 Preheat the grill to high.

3 Put the pork in another large bowl. Form a well in the center of the meat and pour in the egg white mixture. Knead together until well combined. Form 8 patties that are about 1 inch thick and about 2½ inches in diameter.

4 Grill the patties (in batches, if necessary, depending upon the size of your grill) for about 4 minutes, until well browned and cooked through. Serve immediately.

Nutritional values per serving

calories 387; protein 31 g; carbohydrates 11 g; fiber 2 g;
total fat 24 g; saturated fat 9 g; cholesterol 107 mg; sodium 582 mg

Chicken and Sun-Dried Tomato Sausage Patties

Chicken patties are a great way to start the day, especially when they've got a pop of tomato flavor. Sun-dried tomatoes will keep in your cupboard for months, so they can add knockout tomato flavor all year round.

Makes 8 patties; serves 4

2 large egg whites

¼ cup chopped sun-dried tomatoes

¼ cup chopped fresh basil leaves

3 tablespoons grated Parmesan cheese, preferably freshly grated

2 garlic cloves, minced

½ teaspoon salt

½ teaspoon freshly ground black pepper

1 pound ground chicken

1 In a large bowl, beat the egg whites until frothy. Stir in the sun-dried tomatoes, basil, Parmesan, garlic, salt, and pepper.

2 Preheat the grill to high.

3 Put the chicken in another large bowl. Form a well in the center of the meat and pour in the egg white mixture. Knead together until well combined. Form 8 patties that are about 1 inch thick and about 2½ inches in diameter.

4 Grill the patties (in batches, if necessary, depending upon the size of your grill) for about 4 minutes, until well browned and cooked through. Serve immediately.

Nutritional values per serving

calories 162; protein 30 g; carbohydrates 3 g; fiber 1 g;
total fat 3 g; saturated fat 1 g; cholesterol 69 mg; sodium 478 mg

Good Morning Pork and Turkey Sausage Patties

These sausage patties have great texture thanks to the mixture of ground pork and turkey.

Makes 8 patties; serves 4

2 large egg whites

1 small yellow onion, chopped

3 tablespoons chopped fresh sage leaves or 1 teaspoon dried sage

2 garlic cloves, minced

½ teaspoon salt

¼ teaspoon freshly ground black pepper

¼ teaspoon nutmeg

½ pound lean ground pork

½ pound ground turkey

1 In a large bowl, beat the egg whites until frothy. Stir in the onion, sage, garlic, salt, pepper, and nutmeg.

2 Preheat the grill to high.

3 Put the pork and turkey in another large bowl. Form a well in the center of the meat and pour in the egg white mixture. Knead together until well combined. Form 8 patties that are 1 inch thick and about 2½ inches in diameter.

4 Grill the patties (in batches, if necessary, depending upon the size of your grill) for about 4 minutes, until well browned and cooked through. Serve immediately.

Nutritional values per serving

calories 283; protein 28 g; carbohydrates 2 g; fiber 0 g;
total fat 17 g; saturated fat 6 g; cholesterol 95 mg; sodium 114 mg

BACON AND BEYOND ON THE GRILL

With everyone in my family trying to get out to school, to the gym, or off to work, well, mornings can be hectic. But I still want a quick and energizing breakfast for everyone, and that's where the grill comes in handy: it gets bacon or sausage or low-fat, high-flavor breakfast patties ready in just a few minutes.

Bacon Even the most finicky featherweights seem to love bacon, and grilling is the easy, no-bother way to cook it. Set the grill to high and grill the bacon for 7 minutes. Not only is it perfectly crisp, but all the fat is collected in the drip tray, so cleanup is next to nothing. Plus, you don't have to flip bacon in a hot, greasy pan.

Canadian Bacon My boys love Canadian bacon, so we keep plenty of it on hand. They like to pile it on an English muffin with scrambled eggs and some cheddar cheese for their Famous Foreman Big Breakfast Sandwich. Set the grill to medium and grill Canadian bacon for 5 minutes, until it's got a good golden-brown color.

Sausage Links Sausages are another first-round favorite in our house. Brown-and-serve links take only minutes on the grill, and freshly made sausage links from the supermarket can be split lengthwise and grilled until no pink color remains—about 5 minutes. Our supermarket carries packaged fresh links made from pork, chicken, and turkey, with flavorings from apples to sun-dried tomatoes.

Sausage Patties One of the ways I pump up the protein first thing in the morning is with homemade breakfast patties. The night before, I add egg whites to ground chicken or pork to make fresh breakfast patties that I can grill in minutes, sending everyone off with a high-protein start that my family loves. And I do too. See the recipes on the pages that follow.

Smoked Salmon Croque Monsieur

The classic French sandwich, made with ham and Gruyère cheese, is off-the-chart fattening. So we've reworked it to create a still delicious but healthier version that we serve for breakfast or lunch.

Serves 4

8 slices whole wheat bread

4 slices smoked salmon (about 4 ounces)

½ red onion, thinly sliced

½ lemon

½ teaspoon freshly ground black pepper

2 large eggs

1 Preheat the grill to high.

2 Lay 4 slices of the bread on a clean work surface. Arrange the salmon and onion slices on top. Squeeze some lemon juice over the onion and season with the pepper. Close up the sandwiches with the remaining 4 slices bread.

3 Lightly beat the eggs in a wide bowl. Dip both sides of the sandwiches in the egg. Grill (in batches, if necessary, depending upon the size of your grill) for about 3 minutes, until the sandwiches are golden brown. Serve immediately.

Nutritional values per serving
calories 149; protein 12 g; carbohydrates 15 g; fiber 2 g;
total fat 5 g; saturated fat 2 g; cholesterol 119 mg; sodium 537 mg

Tofu "Huevos Rancheros"

I've said it before and I'll say it again: I'm not crazy about tofu. But even a meat eater like me can't argue that it's highly nutritious and grills up beautifully. I'll eat it in this take on the spicy Tex-Mex classic when I want a change from eggs but still need a big shot of protein.

Serves 4

1 cup tomato sauce

1 garlic clove, minced, or ½ teaspoon garlic powder

3 dashes hot sauce

1 pound firm tofu, drained

4 (10-inch) flour tortillas

4 ounces shredded Monterey Jack cheese (1 cup)

1 Mix together the tomato sauce, garlic, and hot sauce in a small bowl.

2 Preheat the grill to high.

3 On a cutting board, cut the tofu into 6 slabs, each approximately ½ inch thick. Pat dry with paper towels. Brush both sides of each piece of tofu with some of the tomato sauce mixture. Grill (in batches, if necessary, depending upon the size of your grill) for 2 minutes. Brush again with a little tomato sauce and grill for 2 minutes more until the tofu has taken on grill marks. Transfer to a platter and cut each piece in half; keep the grill on high.

4 On each tortilla, arrange 3 pieces of cooked tofu near the center. Spoon some of the remaining tomato sauce mixture on top and then sprinkle with the cheese. Roll up the wraps, tucking in the bottoms. Grill for 30 seconds, just until the cheese melts. Serve immediately.

Nutritional values per serving

calories 433; protein 22 g; carbohydrates 49 g; fiber 3 g;
total fat 17 g; saturated fat 1 g; cholesterol 25 mg; sodium 842 mg

Pumpkin French Toast

We love this for special weekend breakfasts when we spend more time than usual enjoying the first meal of the day. Serve with pure maple syrup, honey, or jam, if you'd like. You can also add some bacon to the grill when the French toast is finished, but then be sure to hit the gym!

Serves 4

> 6 large eggs
>
> 3 tablespoons canned pumpkin puree
>
> ½ teaspoon ground cinnamon
>
> ½ teaspoon ground nutmeg
>
> 8 slices white bread
>
> 3 tablespoons walnut pieces

1 Preheat the grill to medium and spray with nonstick cooking spray.

2 Combine the eggs, pumpkin puree, cinnamon, and nutmeg in a wide, shallow bowl and whisk until frothy. Dip the slices of bread into the egg mixture, coating both sides well. Grill (in batches, if necessary, depending upon the size of your grill) for about 3 minutes, until the French toast is crisp and brown on the outside. Sprinkle with the walnuts and serve immediately.

Nutritional values per serving
calories 296; protein 14 g; carbohydrates 28 g; fiber 2 g;
total fat 14 g; saturated fat 3 g; cholesterol 323 mg; sodium 395 mg

Mango Breakfast Parfait

I love talking to butchers—they're a great source of information, telling me what their favorite cuts are to cook on the grill. But it was also a butcher who told me about this great way to prepare fruit for breakfast using the grill and it's a winner: warm grilled mango with cool yogurt, mint, and honey. It's so delicious it's like a breakfast dessert. This makes a fine showing on a Sunday brunch table served in parfait glasses.

Serves 4

> *2 cups low-fat plain yogurt*
>
> *2 ripe mangoes, peeled, halved, and pitted*
>
> *1 tablespoon honey*
>
> *¼ cup walnut pieces*
>
> *1 small handful fresh mint leaves*

1 Preheat the grill to medium.

2 Spoon ½ cup of the yogurt into each of 4 serving bowls or parfait glasses.

3 Brush the mango sections with the honey and grill for about 3 minutes, until they are hot and have taken on grill marks. Transfer to a cutting board and cut the mango into large chunks. Divide the mango among the bowls and top with the remaining yogurt. Sprinkle each serving with some walnuts and a few mint leaves. Serve immediately.

Nutritional values per serving
calories 207; protein 7 g; carbohydrates 34 g; fiber 2 g;
total fat 6 g; saturated fat 1 g; cholesterol 7.5 mg; sodium 78 mg

Sources

For meat

aidells.com
(877) 243-3557
Gourmet, flavored sausages

nimanranch.com
(510) 808-0340
Organic beef, pork, and lamb, including hot dogs and bacon

For seafood

browne-trading.com
(800) 944-7848
Fresh fish and other seafood

legalseafoods.com
(800) 328-3474
Seafood packages (for 2 or 4 people) and fish fillets

For spices, herbs, and seasonings

chefpaul.com
(504) 731-3590
Paul Prudhomme Magic Seasoning Blends, sauces, and marinades

ethnicgrocer.com
(312) 373-1777

kalustyan.com
(908) 688-6111

penzeys.com
(800) 741-7787

For barbecue and hot sauces

elpasochile.com
(888) 472-5727
Tex-Mex marinades and barbecue sauces

mohotta.com
(800) 462-3220
Hot sauces, Jamaican marinades, and spice rubs

For Asian ingredients

orientalpantry.com
(800) 828-0368

uwajimaya.com
(800) 889-1928

For grills and grill accessories

esalton.com
(866) ESALTON
A full line of George Foreman grills, rotisseries, and accessories can be found here and at many retailers nationwide.

Metric Equivalencies

U.S. to metric mass (weight)

1 ounce	28 grams
4 ounces	114 grams
6 ounces	170 grams
8 ounces	227 grams
1 pound (16 ounces)	454 grams
2.2 pounds	1 kilogram

U.S. to metric fluid volume measures

1 teaspoon	5 milliliters
1 tablespoon	15 milliliters
2 tablespoons (1 fluid ounce)	30 milliliters
¼ cup (2 fluid ounces)	60 milliliters
⅓ cup	80 milliliters
½ cup (4 fluid ounces)	120 milliliters
1 cup (8 fluid ounces)	240 milliliters
1 quart (4 cups; 32 fluid ounces)	960 milliliters (.96 liter)

U.S. and British dry volume measures

One 8-ounce U.S. measuring cup = 16 U.S. tablespoons
One 10-ounce British measuring cup = about 21 U.S. tablespoons

U.S. to metric linear measures

¼ inch	6 millimeters
½ inch	12 millimeters
1 inch	2.5 centimeters

Index

Nothing-but-Delicious Sauce, 110–11
nutritional values per serving, 5
nuts, as extra for greatest grilled cheese, 48

O
onions:
    as extra for greatest grilled cheese, 48
    red, grilling, 168
Orange-Peach Glaze, Ham with, 142–43

P
Panini with Pesto Punch, 52
Parfait, Mango Breakfast, 219
pasta, 95
    Penne with Grilled Chicken, Portobellos,
        and Walnuts, 100–101
    Sweet Sausage and Broccoli Rabe with Bow
        Ties, 102–3
pastrami, in Cuban Reuben, 56–57
patties, *see* beef burgers; breakfast patties;
        burgers
Peach-Orange Glaze, Ham with, 142
Peanut Dipping Sauce, 17
Penne with Grilled Chicken, Portobellos, and
        Walnuts, 100–101
pepper(s) (bell):
    Chimichurri Sauce, 138–39
    grilling, 168
    Nothing-but-Delicious Sauce, 110–11
    Red, Chicken Melts, Rancho, 58–59
    Red, Shrimp Quesadillas, Flaming, 32–33
pepper Jack cheese:
    Chicken Quesadillas, 36–37
    Flaming Red Pepper Shrimp Quesadillas,
        32–33
pesto:
    Punch, Panini with, 52
    3 P's Turkey Burger, 86–87
pineapple:
    Avocado Salsa, 42–43
    Frank-'n-, Kebabs, 24–25
    Honey-Glazed, 202–3
pizzas, 95–99

Goat Cheese Garden, 98–99
    guidelines for, 97
    Houston-Not-Hawaii, 96–97
Po'boys, Kid Creole Catfish, 64–65
pool-party tacos, knockout, 39
pork, 125, 134–43
    and Apple Breakfast Patties, 208–9
    Chimichurri, 138–39
    Chops, Apple Cider, 134–35
    Chops, Molasses BBQ, 140–41
    and Grape Kebabs, Grilled, 26–27
    Rolls, Chile-Spiked, 66–67
    sources for, 220
    Tenderloin with Cucumber-Cashew Salad,
        136–37
    and Turkey Sausage Patties, Good Morning,
        212–13
    see also bacon; ham
portobello(s):
    Caps, Stuffed, 178
    Fontina Melts, Open-Faced, 60–61
    Penne with Grilled Chicken, Walnuts and,
        100–101
potato(es):
    Crushed, 186
    Salad, 186
Provolone, Tomato, and Oregano, Grilled,
        50–51
Pumpkin French Toast, 218

Q
quesadillas, 31–38
    Cheddar, with Cherry Tomatoes, 34–35
    Chicken, 36–37
    'Dia Dogs, 38
    Red Pepper Shrimp, Flaming, 32–33

R
Radicchio, Grilled, 174
Rancho Red Pepper Chicken Melts, 58–59
Red Citrus Snapper, 162–63
Reuben, Cuban, 56–57
rubs, *see* spice rubs